THE COMPLETE
Baby and Toddler
Meal Planner

THE COMPLETE
Baby and Toddler Meal Planner

Over 200 quick, easy and healthy recipes

ANNABEL KARMEL

Illustrations by Nadine Wickenden

EBURY PRESS
LONDON

First published in 1991 by Ebury Press
an imprint of Random House UK Ltd
Random House
20 Vauxhall Bridge Road
London SW1V 2SA

10th impression 1996

Editors   Susan Fleming and Fiona Eves
Art Director Elaine Partington

**British Library Cataloguing-in-Publication
Data**

Karmel, Annabel
   The Complete Baby and Toddler Meal Planner:
   Over 200 quick, easy and healthy recipes.
   I. Title
   641.5

   ISBN 0-09-175104-7

AN EDDISON SADD EDITION
Edited, designed and produced by
Eddison Sadd Editions Limited
St Chad's Court, 146B King's Cross Road
London WC1X 9DH

Phototypeset by Wyvern Typesetting Limited,
Bristol, England in Fry's Baskerville and Baskerville No. 2
Origination by Columbia Offset, Hong Kong
Printed in Great Britain by Bath Press Colourbooks, Glasgow

*This book is dedicated
to my children,
Nicholas and Lara
and to the memory of
my first daughter,
Natasha.*

CONTENTS

INTRODUCTION

Like any other besotted young mother, I wanted the very best for my babies. As a food lover and Cordon Bleu cook I wanted them to enjoy the wonderful tastes and aromas of fresh foods. With common sense, extensive research, two cooperative infants and a tolerant husband I knew I could create delicious recipes. Prepared quickly and easily they would be better for babies and toddlers than commercial gluten-free, vitamin- and iron-fortified powders and foods in jars.

The pleasure of seeing my children enjoy my foods has been a wonderful experience. I am reassured to know they are eating good fresh produce not over-processed convenience foods. Why should I feed my children from packets and jars when I would never give them to my husband or friends?

From six months babies have excellent taste buds and can appreciate a wide range of foods. This book will help you give your babies a healthy eating pattern for life. Instead of bland purées and sickly sweet desserts your children can enjoy a wide variety of tasty, wholesome dishes. Indeed, most of the recipes for toddlers can be enjoyed by the whole family.

All paediatricians and child nutritionists have their own theories and the more people you ask, the more muddled you become. No wonder mothers turn to commercial baby food. However, a report in April 1991 by The Food Commission found that as many as 40 per cent of shop-bought baby foods failed to meet with minimum nutrient levels that doctors have recommended. Added water and thickeners are used to bulk out small amounts of basic ingredients. There is also no indication on the labelling of baby foods as to the amount of each ingredient. Only 2 out of 22 meat-based baby foods provided more than 20 per cent meat and some well known brands as little as 4 per cent meat. Some 'low-sugar' rusks contained more sugar than a doughnut. Believe me, there is no mystique to feeding babies and toddlers and the benefit of home-cooked food is that you know exactly what ingredients your child is eating.

This book is for mothers who want their babies and toddlers to eat well and enjoy their food. The majority of recipes are easily made and do not need hours in the kitchen. The longer you spend cooking the more fractious you feel when your child refuses food. With a liquidiser or food processor and ice-cube trays a month's supply can be prepared in one morning. Liquidise a variety of foods and freeze them as purée ice-cubes. Simply defrost them as needed for an instant, freshly prepared meal. If your baby won't eat, little time has been wasted so you will not feel too offended

I give guidelines but there are no hard and fast rules to feeding a baby. Babies under one year should not have salt added to their food; salt in moderation after this will do no harm. Restricting salt intake may reduce the incidence of hypertension in later life. When possible I cook for the whole family and I believe most husbands would not appreciate unseasoned chicken, bland swede and unsweetened apple crumble.

If there are rules – and rules are made to be broken – they are to aim for:

1. Fresh food
2. Low animal fat
3. Low sugar
4. Low salt (No salt before one year)

A baby in the home is an opportunity to look at the dietary rules for the whole family. Some of these recipes are so delicious I serve them when entertaining! Babies' nutrition in their first year probably has greater influence than at any other time of life. This reinforces the need to start early with a good balanced diet. When your child opts for the raw fruits and vegetables, which adults imagine kids hate, over sugary sweets you will recognise your success.

Good luck, I hope you and your child enjoy many happy meals together!

CHAPTER ONE

THE BEST FIRST FOODS FOR YOUR BABY

Many mothers feel that, once their baby is three months old, they should be starting to feed him solids. In fact there is no 'right' age as every baby is different.

Physiologically, there is no rush to get your baby started on solids. A baby's digestive system is not fully matured for the first few months and foreign proteins very early on may increase the likelihood of allergic food problems later. However, be warned, socially there is a kind of competitive spirit amongst mothers to get their child on to puréed steak and chips as soon as possible! I would advise that, provided your child is satisfied and growing properly, you should wait until he is between four and six months old before starting to give him simple solid foods.

Milk is Still the Major Food

It is very important to remember when starting your baby on solids that milk is still the most natural and the best food for growing babies. I would encourage mothers to try breast-feeding. Apart from the emotional benefits, breast milk contains antibodies that help protect infants from infection. In the first few months, they are particularly vulnerable and the colostrum a mother produces in the first few days of breast-feeding is a very important source of antibodies which help to build up a baby's immune system. (If only for this reason, it is obvious that there are enormous benefits in breast-feeding your child even for as little as one week.) It is also medically proven that breast-fed babies are less likely to develop certain diseases in later life.

Milk should contain all the nutrients that your baby needs to grow. There are 65 calories in 100 ml/4 fl oz of milk and formula milk is fortified with vitamins and iron. Cow's milk is not such a 'complete' food for human babies so is best not started until your baby is one year old.

Solids are introduced to add *bulk* to a baby's diet, and to introduce new tastes, textures and aromas; they also help the baby to practise using the muscles in his mouth. But giving a baby too much solid food too early may lead to constipation, and fewer nutrients than he needs. It would be very difficult for a baby to get the equivalent amount of nutrients from the small amount of solids as he gets from his milk.

Do not use softened water when making up your baby's bottle or repeatedly boiled water because of the danger of concentrating mineral salts. Babies' bottles should not be warmed in a microwave, as the milk may be too hot even though the bottle feels cool to the touch. Warm bottles standing in hot water.

There is no fixed rule as to how much milk a baby should consume during the day. However, it is important to make sure (especially as it is highly likely that a bottle may not be finished at each feed) that up to the age of five months, your baby drinks milk at least four times a day. If the number of feeds is reduced too quickly, your baby will not be able to drink as much as is needed. Some mothers make the mistake of giving their baby solid food when he or she is hungry, when what he really needs is an additional milk feed.

Although most babies of six months are perfectly able to drink pasteurised cow's milk and many mothers, especially in other countries, start their babies on cow's milk this early, it is best to continue with breast or formula milk for one year.

Dairy products like yoghurt, *Petit Suisse* and cheese can be introduced any time after six months and are generally very popular with babies. Choose whole milk products as opposed to low-fat.

Fresh is Best

Fresh foods just *do* taste, smell and look better than jars of pre-prepared baby foods. Neither is there any doubt that, prepared correctly, they are better for your baby (and you), for it is inevitable nutrients, especially vitamins, are lost in the processing of pre-prepared baby foods. Home-made food tastes quite different from the jars you can buy. (If you were ever to try a blind tasting of popular brands of baby foods, you would know that it is very difficult to recognise what particular food each jar contains!)

There is also a very limited variety of single fruit and vegetables. Most of the jars available contain bland combinations of foods puréed to the same consistency so that it is difficult for your child to differentiate one food from another. It can be quite a problem getting your baby to accept the coarser texture of home-made purées once he is used to the very smooth texture of commercially prepared baby foods. It's best therefore to start cooking for your baby yourself right from the beginning. I believe your child is less likely to become a fussy eater if he is used to a wide selection of tastes and textures from a very early age. You can 'train' your child to enjoy the flavours of fresh spinach or apple and pea purée rather than crave sweets and doughnuts. Why give them sugary and fatty foods when healthy food can be just as enjoyable?

Your Baby's Nutritional Requirements

The following six are essential nutrients that a child needs for a healthy diet and to promote growth.

PROTEINS

Proteins are needed for the growth and repair of our bodies, any extra can be used to provide energy (or is deposited as fat).

Proteins are made up of different amino acids. Some foods; meat, fish, dairy produce, including cheeses, and soya beans, contain all the amino acids that are essential to our bodies. Other foods; grains, pulses, nuts and seeds, are still valuable sources of protein but do not contain all the essential amino acids.

CARBOHYDRATES

Carbohydrates and fat provide our bodies with their main source of energy. The former also provide fibre which adds bulk to our diet and acts as a natural laxative.

There are two types of carbohydrate,

sugar is one and starch (which in complex form provides fibre) is the other. In both types there are two forms – the natural and the refined. In both cases, it is the natural form which provides a more healthy alternative.

SUGARS
Natural
Fruit and Fruit juices
Vegetables
Vegetable juices
Refined
Sugars and honey
Soft drinks
Sweet jellies
Jams and other preserves
Cakes and biscuits

STARCHES
Natural
Whole-grain breakfast cereals, flour, bread and pasta
Brown rice
Potatoes
Dried beans and lentils
Peas, bananas and many other fruits and vegetables
Refined
Processed breakfast cereals (i.e. sugar-coated flakes)
White flour, breads and pasta
White rice
Sugary biscuits
Cakes

FATS

Fats provide a concentrated source of energy. The body also needs to store some fat to prevent excessive loss of body heat. Thus a certain amount of fat is essential in everyone's diet. Foods that contain fats also contain the fat-soluble vitamins A, D, E and K. The problem is that many people eat too much fat and the wrong type of fat.

There are two types of fat – saturated, which mainly comes from animal sources, and unsaturated which comes from vegetable sources. It is the saturated fats which are the most harmful and which may lead to high cholesterol levels and coronary disease later in life.

It is important to give your baby whole milk for at least the first three years but try to reduce fats in cooking and use butter and margarine in moderation. Try to reduce saturated fats in your child's diet by cutting down on red meat, especially fatty meats like lamb; replace with more chicken and fish. This may in fact be a good time to review the whole family's eating habits, and to cut out all that butter on Daddy's toast in the morning!

VITAMINS

The possibility of vitamin deficiencies in the developed world should not be ignored. The children most at risk are those who follow a Vegan diet (i.e. no animal products at all) and those drinking cow's milk from the age of six months. Paediatricians recommend that these children should take a daily vitamin supplement until they are at least two.

For most children eating fresh food in sufficient quantity and drinking formula milk until the age of one year, vitamin supplements are probably unnecessary.

There are two types of vitamins – water-soluble (C and B complex) and fat-soluble (A, D, E and K). Water-soluble vitamins cannot be stored by the body so foods containing these should be eaten daily. They can also easily be destroyed by overcooking, especially when fruit and vegetables are boiled in water. You should try to preserve these vitamins by eating the foods raw or just lightly cooked (in a steamer, for instance).

There is some controversy over

FATS

Saturated
Butter
Meat
Lard, suet and dripping
Eggs
Cheese and full-fat yoghurt
Cakes and biscuits
Hard margarine
Whole milk
Unsaturated fats
Sunflower, grapeseed, safflower, sesame, soya, rapeseed and olive oils
Soft polyunsaturated margarine
Oily fish (e.g. mackerel)

VITAMIN A

Essential for growth, healthy skin, tooth enamel and good vision.

Liver
Oily fish
Carrots
Dark green vegetables (e.g. broccoli)
Sweet potatoes
Oranges
Squash
Tomatoes
Lentils
Watercress
Apricots and peaches
Whole milk and eggs
Butter and margarine

VITAMIN B COMPLEX

Essential for growth, changing food into energy, for a healthy nervous system and as an aid to digestion. There are a large number of vitamins in the B group. Some are found in many foods, but no foods except for liver and yeast extract contain them all.

Meat, especially meat juices (so use in gravy) and liver
Fish
Dairy produce and eggs
Whole-grain cereals
Wheatgerm
Dark green vegetables
Potatoes
Yeast extract (e.g. Marmite)
Nuts
Dried beans
Bananas

VITAMIN C

Is needed for growth, healthy tissue and healing of wounds. It helps in the absorption of iron.

Vegetables such as: broccoli; Brussels sprouts; greens; sweet peppers; potatoes; spinach; cauliflower.
Fruits such as: oranges and other citrus fruits; blackcurrants; melon; papaya; strawberries and tomatoes

VITAMIN D

Essential for proper bone formation, it works in conjunction with calcium. It is found in few foods, but is made by the skin in the presence of *sunlight*.

Oily fish
Liver
Oils
Eggs
Margarine
Dairy produce

VITAMIN E

Important for the composition of the cell structure, and helps the body to create and maintain red blood cells.

Vegetable oils
Margarine
Wheatgerm
Nuts

VITAMIN K

Aids in blood clotting, maintains bones and is present in the intestine.
It is found in most vegetables and whole-grain cereals.

whether vitamin supplements can improve your child's IQ. As vitamins are necessary for the correct development of the brain and nervous system, it is important that a good supply of all vitamins is taken. However, a good balanced diet should supply all that is required and an excess of vitamins is potentially harmful. Good sources of all the major vitamins and minerals are given in the tables to the left.

CALCIUM

Calcium is needed for strong bones, good teeth and growth.

Dairy produce, especially milk
Canned fish with bones (e.g. sardines, but only for older children)
Dried fruit
Bread and flour
Broccoli
Pulses

IRON

Iron is needed for healthy blood and muscles. A deficiency in iron is probably the most common and will leave your child feeling tired and run down.

Liver and red meat
Oily fish
Egg yolks
Dried fruits (especially apricots)
Whole-grain cereals
Lentils and dried beans
Green leafy vegetables
Chocolate

WATER

Humans can survive for quite a time without food, but only a few days without water. Babies lose more water through their kidneys and skin than adults and also through vomiting and diarrhoea.

Thus it is very important that your baby should not be allowed to dehydrate. Make sure he drinks plenty of fluids. Cool, boiled water is the best drink to give your baby on hot days particularly, as it will cool the body down quicker than any sugary drink.

It is really not necessary to give a very young baby anything to drink other than milk or plain water if he is just thirsty. Fruit syrups, squashes and sweetened herbal drinks should be discouraged to prevent dental decay. Don't be fooled if the packet says 'dextrose' – this is just a type of sugar.

If your baby refuses to drink water then give him unsweetened baby juice or fresh 100 per cent fruit juices. Dilute according to instructions or for fresh juice use one part juice to three parts water, gradually increasing to half and half.

The Question of Allergies

It is fairly common for babies to inherit food allergies from their parents, and where there is a history of a particular food allergy, that food should only be introduced singly and with great care.

The commonest foods which carry a

risk of allergic reaction in babies are cow's milk and dairy products, eggs, fish (especially shellfish), some fruits, nuts and foods containing gluten. Some babies (and older children) can also react to artificial food colourings and additives. The commonest allergic problems which may be triggered by adverse reactions to food are: nausea; vomiting; diarrhoea; asthma; eczema; hayfever; rashes and swelling of the eyes, lips and face. This is one reason it is unwise to rush starting your baby on solid foods.

There is no need to be unduly worried about food allergy, unless there is a family history. The incidence of food allergy in normal babies is extremely small and, with the tendency to a later introduction of solid food between four and six months, they have become even less common. However, it is still children under the age of eighteen months who are most likely to develop an allergy to a particular food. Although a lot of children 'grow out of it' by the age of two, some food allergies – particularly a sensitivity to eggs, milk, shellfish or nuts – can last for life. If your child has an allergy, do tell friends' mums and the school when he is old enough.

Never be afraid to take your baby to the doctor if you are worried that there is something wrong. Young babies' immune systems are not fully matured and babies can become ill very quickly if they are not treated properly and can develop serious complications.

LACTOSE INTOLERANCE

Lactose intolerance is not actually an allergy. Children who suffer lactose intolerance lack the substance lactase, an enzyme present in the superficial layers of the small bowel, which breaks lactose down to simpler sugars. Lactose is present in all milks and these babies will not be able to drink breast or cow's milk. A soya formula is given.

Some children who are lactose intolerant are able to eat dairy products like cheese and yoghurt with no ill effects.

COW'S MILK PROTEIN ALLERGY

If your baby is sensitive to cow's milk, consult your doctor who will probably recommend a soya-based milk formula. Unmodified soya milk is not suitable as it is nutritionally inadequate. However, some babies who are allergic to cow's milk are also allergic to soya-based milks and for those babies there are a number of hypo-allergic milk formulae available on prescription. Breast milk is the best milk for babies who are allergic to cow's milk but mothers may need to limit dairy foods themselves as these can be transferred to their baby through breast milk.

No dairy products are tolerated in this condition and in the weaning diet milk-free vegetable or soya margarine may be substituted for butter and carob for milk chocolate. Very often babies outgrow this allergy by the age of two.

EGGS

Avoid giving egg whites before one year. Cooked egg yolks may be given once the baby is well established in mixed feeding, between eight and nine months.

FISH

Most paediatricians advise mothers not to give fish to their babies before eight months and to avoid all shellfish.

FRUITS

Some children can have an adverse reaction to citrus and berry fruits. Rosehip or blackcurrant are good Vitamin-C-rich alternatives to orange.

NUTS

Nuts, even ground, should be avoided for at least the first seven months. Children under three can choke on whole nuts.

GLUTEN

If there is a family history of gluten intolerance babies under six months must follow a gluten-free diet but it is preferable for all young babies. Gluten is found

in wheat, rye, barley and oats and gluten sensitivity can cause coeliac disease which, although rare can be serious.

When buying baby cereals and rusks, choose varieties that are gluten-free. Baby rice is the safest to try at first and thereafter there are plenty of alternative gluten-free products such as soya, corn, rice, millet and potato flours for thickening and baking, brown rice, rice noodles, buckwheat spaghetti etc.

Preparing Baby Foods

Preparing and cooking baby foods is not difficult, but because you are dealing with a young baby, considerations like hygiene must be of the utmost importance.

EQUIPMENT

Most of the equipment needed will already be in your kitchen – mashers, graters, sieves etc – but the following three pieces I consider are vital!

Mouli This hand-turned food mill with variable cutting discs purées the food, separating it from the seeds and skin which can be difficult for the baby to digest. It is best used for fruit, vegetables, fish and the softer textured meats such as chicken and liver.

Blender or food processor This is useful for puréeing larger quantities. However, foods for young babies will often need to be sieved afterwards to remove any seeds and skin.

Steamer The best way to preserve the fresh taste and vitamins in fruits and vegetables is to cook them in a steamer. It is worth buying a good multi-tiered steamer which will enable you to cook several different foods at the same time. (A colander over a saucepan along with a well-fitting lid, is a cheaper alternative.)

STERILISING

At first, it is very important to sterilise bottles, and particularly, the teats that your baby sucks, properly by whatever approved method you choose. Warm milk is the perfect breeding ground for bacteria and if bottles are not properly washed and sterilised, your baby can become very ill. It is also best to sterilise the dishes and spoons you use for feeding your baby. It would be impossible, however, to sterilise *all* the equipment you use for cooking and puréeing baby food, but take extra care to keep everything very clean.

Use a dishwasher if you have one; the water is at a much higher temperature than it would be possible to use if washing the utensils by hand and helps to sterilise your equipment. However, once it is removed from the dishwasher, it does not remain sterile; bottles should be filled with milk immediately and stored in the fridge. Dry utensils with kitchen paper rather than a non-sterile tea towel.

Milk bottles should continue to be sterilised until your baby is one year old, but there is really not much point sterilis-ing spoons or food containers beyond the age when your baby crawls and puts everything in reach into his mouth.

COOKING BABY FOODS

Fruit and vegetables can lose nutrients when they are cooked so it makes sense to eat some both cooked and raw. However, raw ones would be difficult to digest for a young baby so, until the age of six months, most fruit and vegetables (apart from ripe bananas) should be cooked. As the baby gains teeth and learns to chew, the fruit or vegetables can be cooked more lightly in order to retain Vitamin C and crispness. After about six months, your baby can have purées of raw fruit and fresh grated fruit; raw or very *al dente* vegetables can be given as a finger food.

Cook in many ways – boiling, steaming, stewing or baking. Try to avoid fat-based methods of cooking such as frying (or cut down on the amount of fat used). Steaming, as mentioned above, is by far the best and, to maximise on nutritional benefits, the water in which or over which vegetables have cooked (so long as it does not contain salt) could be used as a drink or as the cooking water for something else such as pasta. Try also to maximise on fuel economy; steam a number of different foods at one time before puréeing and storing separately.

Cook fruit and vegetable purées for your baby by whichever method you choose. In each case make sure the purée is completely smooth, with no lumps. Later on you can adjust the texture of the purée to suit your baby as he starts to chew. Freeze any purée you are not using straightaway.

Boiling or steaming Wash fruit or vegetable carefully, peel, seed or stone as necessary and cut into small pieces. Add just enough water to cover and simmer until tender or steam (about 10 minutes, see individual recipes). Drain or remove from steamer, retaining the cooking water, then blend, mouli or mash, adding some of the cooking water to bring it to the correct consistency for your baby.

Microwaving Peel, seed or stone the fruit or vegetable as necessary and cut into slices. Put in a microwave dish with enough water just to cover and cover the dish with a lid. Microwave on High for about 3 minutes. Uncover, stir, re-cover and cook for another 2 minutes or until tender. Cooking times will vary according to how hard the fruit is to begin with. Blend, mash or mouli to the right consistency, adding water as necessary.

FREEZING BABY FOODS

Whenever possible, prepare more food than is immediately needed and freeze the remainder in ice-cube trays for future meals. There are a limited number of foods that do not freeze well (like bananas and avocados) but most foods can be frozen with excellent results. Thus, in one or two hours a week, you can prepare enough to feed your baby for a month – making for a happier mother and baby and more time to spend together.

You will need a freezer which can freeze food to 0°F(−18°C) or below in 24 hours and sterile packaging. At the earliest stages, when only teaspoons of food are being taken, this means plastic ice-cube trays (sterilise these as well) and polythene freezer bags.

Cook and purée the food as described in the recipes, cover, leave to cool, then freeze until hard in ice-cube trays. Knock out and store in clearly labelled freezer bags. Label the food with the expiry date so you never give your baby food that is past its best.

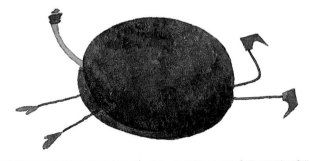

FREEZER STORAGE TIMES

Fruits	6 months
Vegetables	6 months
Purées with milk	4–6 weeks
Fish	10 weeks
Meat and chicken	10 weeks

Apple, pear, banana, papaya	4–5 months
Carrot, cauliflower, potato, courgette, squash, green beans, swede, sweet potato	4–5 months
Dried fruit, peach, kiwi, apricot, plum, melon, avocado	5–6 months
Peas, tomato, spinach, celery, leek, sweet pepper	5–6 months
Chicken, dairy products	6 months
Other meats	6–12 months
Foods containing gluten	6 months
Citrus fruit, berries, mango	6–7 months
Split pea, butter beans, lentils	8–9 months
Eggs	8–9 months
Fish	8–9 months
Shellfish	over 2 years

To thaw one meal, remove the relevant number of cubes of food from the bag (only one at the very beginning) and leave at room temperature for an hour. Heat thoroughly, cool, then serve immediately. If using a microwave, stir well to make sure there is an even distribution of heat, allow to cool. Always test the temperature of food before giving it to your baby. Fruits to be served cold can defrost in the refrigerator overnight.

Never re-freeze foods which have already been frozen, and never reheat them more than once.

When can they have . . .?

I have listed above right when you should introduce particular foods to your baby. This is not an exhaustive list and you should refer to each chapter for more information.

Meal Planners

In the next chapter I have devised some meal planners which will help you through the first weeks when you start to wean your baby. There are endless variations on the foods that can be given and the order in which they can be introduced.

If your baby's last meal is close to bed time, avoid giving him anything heavy or difficult to digest. This is certainly not the time to experiment with new foods if you both want a good night's sleep.

I have tried to give a wide choice of recipes, although I would expect that in practice meals that your baby enjoys would be repeated several times over the period of a week – and this is where your freezer will come in handy.

In each subsequent chapter, there are meal planners for your baby which you may follow or simply use as a guide. Adapt the charts according to what is in season and what you are preparing for your family. From nine months onwards, you should be able to cook for your baby and family together, perhaps eating the recipes you give your baby for lunch and tea for your own supper.

In these later charts, I have set out four meals a day. However, many babies are quite satisfied with three meals and some healthy snacks.

Many of the vegetable purées in the early chapters can be transformed into a vegetable soup; and a number of the vegetable dishes can serve as good side dishes for the family. If you give the baby some of the vegetables you are preparing for the family, make sure they have not been salted. In the later chapters many recipes are suitable for the whole family.

After each recipe you will find a symbol of two faces, one smiling, the other gloomy, each with a tick box. You will find these useful in recording the success (or otherwise) of your baby meal recipes!

CHAPTER TWO

FOUR TO SIX MONTHS AND WEANING

In the recent past there was a lot of pressure on parents to start their babies on solid food much earlier than four months – this pressure was variously commercial, medical and social (keeping up with the Jones's baby!). Ideas have now changed and this is all to the good, for many quite ordinary foods, as already discussed, can cause allergies. Neither is a baby's digestive system capable, until at least three months old, of absorbing foods more complex than baby milk.

When to Start Weaning

Every baby is different and some larger babies may just not be getting enough to satisfy them. Your baby will let you know when she needs to start solids; if, for example, she is no longer satisfied after a 250 ml/8 fl oz bottle; if the interval between feeds becomes shorter over a prolonged period or if she starts becoming unsettled during the night. Another sure sign is when she reaches out and tries to chew everything in sight!

The First Solid Foods

'Solids' is a strange word to use for the mush we give to our babies and it is a little misleading.

Try only *one food at a time* at the very beginning. Offer apple purée for instance for a couple of days before giving her pear or banana. In that way, if there is a reaction, you will know what caused it. Later on, you can make it all more interesting by *combining* different foods.

The other vital point is that you *should not reduce the milk intake.* Milk is still the most important factor in her growth and development.

On pages 38–41 I have set out some feeding charts which will help you when you start to wean your baby. Use these charts as a guide, adapting them according to what is in season and what you are preparing for your family.

RICE

Initially I should advise one of the commercial baby rice cereals. These, although refined, are enriched with vitamins and they should also be free of sugar and salt. (This information will be printed on the packet and in fact this is a good time to start reading the lists of contents of all packets, jars and cans to look out for undesirables.) Baby rice is also easily digested. Make it up with baby milk or boiled cooled water according to the instructions on the packet.

FRUIT

Since most babies are born with a 'sweet tooth' (breast milk is naturally sweet), you should have no trouble in getting your baby to enjoy eating fruit. Fruit that is fully ripe is naturally sweet. If you think a purée is sour-tasting, you can add a little honey or some apple juice. Remember though, that the baby may actually prefer something less sweet than you and that is all to the good!

Most fruits provide Vitamin C and minerals and the yellow fruits contain Vitamin A. At first a baby should have cooked purées of fruits like apples and pears; ripe bananas are the only fruit that can be eaten raw at this stage. At about six months, your baby can graduate to raw mashed fruits; pears, papaya, melon, peaches, grapes and plums are all delicious as long as they are ripe.

Fresh fruits are best but fruits canned

in their own juice or water (*not* in a syrup) could also be used. Dried fruits should be introduced later and in small quantities; although they are nutritious they tend to be a laxative.

VEGETABLES

Some people prefer to start their babies on vegetables rather than fruit. Because most babies will take to eating fruit quite happily, they feel it is important to establish a liking for more savoury tastes.

Vegetables contain Vitamins A, C, E and K, as well as various minerals of value to a growing baby. Different vegetables provide different food values – green, Vitamin C, yellow, Vitamin A, for instance – so a variety is of value at later stages. At the beginning, though, when just introducing a baby to solids, it is best to start with root vegetables, particularly carrots, since they are naturally sweet.

Many vegetables have quite strong flavours – broccoli for instance – so when solids are fairly well established, you could mix in some potato to make it more palatable. Very young babies like their food quite bland.

Textures

At the very beginning of weaning, the rice and fruit or vegetable purées should be fairly wet and soft. This means that most vegetables, for instance, should be cooked until very soft so that they purée easily. You will probably need to thin out the consistency of the purées since babies are more likely to accept food in a semi-liquid form. You can use formula or breast milk, fruit juice or boiled water.

As your baby becomes more accustomed to the feel of 'solid food' in her mouth, you can gradually reduce the amount of liquid that you add to the purées, which will encourage her to chew a little. This should be a natural process as she should want to chew her food as she starts teething (usually between six and twelve months). You could also *thicken* the purées if necessary with baby rice or some crumbled rusk. As the baby becomes older and solid feeding is established (at the age of about six months), some fruit can be served raw and vegetables can be cooked more lightly (retaining more Vitamin C). Food can also be mashed or finely chopped to encourage chewing later on.

Remember to peel, core and seed fruits as necessary before cooking and/or purée-ing (or put them through a mouli). Vegetables with fibres or seeds should be sieved or put through a mouli for a smooth texture. The husks of leguminous vegetables cannot be digested at this stage.

Quantities

At the very beginning, don't expect your baby to take more than 1–2 teaspoons of her baby rice or a fruit or vegetable purée. For this you should need 1 portion – in this section, this means a cube from an ice-cube tray. This is approximately 1 tablespoon in volume, but you'll need this much because of spitting and spills!

By the time your baby is six months, she could have graduated to eating 1–2 tablespoons of solids at each meal, which means defrosting *two* frozen food-cubes of the same food.

Drinks

Water, as outlined on page 13, is the best drink to offer. But freshly squeezed citrus fruits, particularly orange, have a good nutritional value, being high in Vitamin C. Dilute with an equal amount of cooled boiled water. (Never boil citrus juices or they lose their vitamin content.) Apple juice is not so high in Vitamin C as orange juice but is still a good drink. (If your baby reacts to citrus fruit juice, offer blackcurrant or rosehip.)

If buying commercial fruit juices, they should be unsweetened. The bottled fruit juices for babies need to be well diluted according to the label instructions.

A juicer is a useful machine to have in the kitchen when there is a baby in the house. Many fruits *and* vegetables can be turned into nutritious drinks.

TIPS FOR INTRODUCING SOLIDS

1 Make the rice or purée fairly wet and soft at first, using breast or formula milk, an unsweetened juice or cooking water. A handy tip is to mix the purée in the plastic removable top of a feeding bottle (which has been sterilised).

2 Hold your baby comfortably in the feeding position and relax. It would be better if *both* of you were protected against spills!

3 Choose a time when your baby is not frantically hungry and give her some milk first to partially satisfy her – she will then be more receptive to the new idea.

4 Babies are unable to lick food off a spoon with their tongues, so choose a small, *shallow* plastic teaspoon off which she can take some food with her lips. (Special weaning spoons can be bought.)

5 Start by giving just one solid feed during the day, about 1–2 teaspoons to begin with. I prefer to give this feed at lunchtime.

FRUIT AND VEGETABLES

FOUR TO FIVE MONTHS

Apple

Choose a sweet variety of eating apple. Peel, halve, core and slice 2 medium apples. Put into a heavy saucepan with enough water to cover and cook over a low heat until soft (about 10 minutes). Or steam over water for the same length of time. Purée.

Apple and Cinnamon

Simmer 2 apples in apple juice with a cinnamon stick. Cook as above, remove stick before puréeing.

MAKES 5 PORTIONS

Pear

Peel, halve and core 2 pears, then cut into small pieces. Cover with a little water, cook over a low heat until soft (about 8 minutes). Or steam over water for the same length of time. Purée.

When your baby is six months or older, there is no longer any need to cook the pear before making it into a purée, provided that the fruit is ripe.

MAKES 5 PORTIONS

Banana

This is the first uncooked fruit that a baby should be given. Use a very ripe banana. Use 4 cm/1½ inches and mash very well with a fork to make it as smooth as possible. Add a little boiled water or baby milk if it is too thick and sticky for your baby to swallow.

If the banana is not ripe enough, split the skin and heat it in the oven or microwave for a couple of minutes to ripen before preparing.

Do not freeze bananas.

MAKES 1 PORTION

Papaya

Papaya is an excellent fruit to give a very young baby. It has a pleasing sweet taste which is not too strong and blends within seconds to a perfect texture.

Cut a medium fruit in half, remove all the black seeds and scoop out the flesh. Steam for 3–5 minutes, then purée.

When your baby is over six months, papaya may be eaten raw.

MAKES 4 PORTIONS

Cream of Fruit

Combining a fruit purée with baby milk and baby rice or crumbled rusk can make it more palatable for your baby. In the next few months, when your baby may start eating some other exotic fruits like mango and kiwi, this method of 'diluting' the fruit purée with milk will also make them less acidic.

Peel, core, steam or boil and purée the fruit as described and, for each 4-portion quantity of prepared fruit, stir in 1 tablespoon unflavoured baby rice or half a low-sugar rusk and 2 tablespoons baby milk.

MAKES 3 EXTRA PORTIONS

Three-Fruit Purée

This is a delicious combination of three of the first fruits that your baby can eat.

Mix 1 dessertspoon each of pear and apple purées (see page 24) with half a banana, mashed. Later (after six months), you can use half a raw ripe pear, peeled, cored and cut into chunks. Put this and the half banana through a mouli to make a smooth purée, then mix together with the dessertspoon of cooked apple purée.

MAKES 4 PORTIONS

Carrot

Small thin carrots are sweetest, so choose these if possible.

Peel, trim and slice 2 medium carrots. Either steam the carrot slices until tender (15 minutes), or boil in about 175 ml/6 fl oz boiling water (about 10 minutes). Purée in a food processor, blender or mouli until the desired consistency. Add cooled boiled water, a teaspoon at a time to the steamed vegetable to make a smooth purée. Drain the boiled vegetable, reserving the cooking liquid and add as much of this as is necessary to make the desired consistency. (As the baby gets older, there should be no need to add any extra water.)

The cooking time is longer for small babies. Once your baby can chew, cut the time down to preserve Vitamin C and keep the vegetables crisper.

MAKES 4
PORTIONS

Swede, Turnip and Parsnip

Use half a swede or 100 g/4 oz of turnip or parsnip. Scrub, peel and cut into small cubes. Cover with 175 ml/6 fl oz boiling water and simmer, covered, until tender (about 20 minutes). Drain, reserving the cooking liquid and mash well with a fork.

MAKES 4 PORTIONS

Butternut Squash

Butternut squashes are the same shape as avocado pears. They have a hard peach-coloured skin, orange flesh and a lovely sweet taste.

Peel and halve a small butternut squash, weighing about 100 g/4 oz. Remove seeds and cut the flesh into 2.5 cm/1 inch cubes. Steam until tender (about 8 minutes). Transfer to a blender and process until a purée of the desired consistency.

MAKES 4 PORTIONS

Green Beans

Top, tail, remove any stringy bits and cut 100 g/4 oz beans diagonally into thin slices. Steam until tender (about 8–10 minutes), then put in a blender and process. Add a little boiled water or baby milk to make a smooth purée. Any variety of green bean is suitable but smaller, younger beans are more tender. Later on whole beans make great finger food with a sauce (See Green Fingers page 92).

Broccoli and Cauliflower

Use 100 g/4 oz of either. Wash well, cut into small florets and add 150 ml/5 fl oz boiling water. Simmer, covered, until tender (about 10–15 minutes). Drain, reserving the cooking liquid. Put through a mouli, adding a little of the reserved liquid (or baby milk) to make the purée the desired consistency.

Or steam the florets for 15 minutes for better flavour and retention of nutrients. Once your baby has teeth and can chew, cut the time down to 8–10 minutes to keep the vegetables crisp. Add boiled water or baby milk to make a smooth purée.

MAKES 4 PORTIONS

Courgette

Wash 2 medium courgettes carefully, remove the ends and slice. (The skin is soft, so does not need to be removed.) Steam until tender (about 10–15 minutes), then put through a mouli or mash with a fork. (No need to add extra liquid.)
MAKES 8 PORTIONS

Potato

Carefully wash a 100 g/4 oz potato, removing any blemishes from the skin, then cover with 120 ml/4 fl oz boiling water and simmer until tender (about 20–30 minutes). Peel off the skin, then mash until smooth. Add enough baby milk to make the purée the desired consistency.

Alternatively, bake a potato in the oven preheated to 400°F(200° C)Gas 6 for about 1 hour or until soft. Scoop out the inside and mash with a little baby milk. (Later on, keep the baked potato skins, as they are very good for babies to chew on when teething.)

Save fuel and time by cooking these with the family meal or cook many more portions. Small quantities are most economically cooked in the microwave.
MAKES 5 PORTIONS

Cream of Carrot Purée

A creamy purée can be made with many different vegetables by adding milk and baby rice. Make a purée with 75 g/3 oz of carrot (page 25). Mix 2–3 teaspoons unflavoured baby rice with 175 ml/6 fl oz warm baby milk. Vary the amount of rice according to how thick you want the purée. Stir the baby rice mixture into the vegetable purée. Half a low-sugar rusk mixed with milk will also make a creamy purée. Allow the rusk to soften in the baby milk before mixing it into the vegetable purée of your choice.
MAKES 12 PORTIONS

Potato, Courgette and Green Beans

Combining potato with green vegetables makes them more palatable for your baby. Peel and chop a medium potato. Boil in water below a steamer for 35 minutes until soft. Steam 25 g/1 oz trimmed and sliced green beans with 1 trimmed and sliced courgette above the potato for the last 10 minutes of cooking time. Drain the potato and purée with the other vegetables in a mouli.
MAKES 7 PORTIONS

Broccoli Trio

Potato is such a good addition to green vegetables, making them more palatable for your baby. Boil a medium potato in the water below a steamer for 35 minutes until soft. Steam 50 g/2 oz of broccoli and the same of cauliflower florets above the potato for the last 10 minutes. When all the vegetables are tender, purée them in a blender with a dessertspoon of baby milk.

MAKES 14 PORTIONS

Carrot and Cauliflower Purée

Combining vegetables makes them more interesting and once your baby has got used to carrot and cauliflower separately, this combination makes a nice change. Cook 50 g/2 oz carrots, scraped and sliced, in boiling water for 20 minutes until soft. After 10 minutes, add 175 g/6 oz cauliflower florets. Drain the vegetables and purée in a mouli. Stir in 2 tablespoons baby milk.

MAKES 8 PORTIONS

FRUIT AND VEGETABLES

FIVE TO SIX MONTHS

Peach

Bring a small saucepan of water to the boil. Cut a shallow cross on the skin of 2 peaches, submerge them in the water for 1 minute, then plunge into cold water. Skin the peaches and chop, discarding the stones. Steam the peaches until tender (about 5 minutes), purée.

Prepare fresh apricots in the same way. Both can be eaten raw, if ripe, after six months.

MAKES 4 PORTIONS

Cantaloupe Melon

Cantaloupes are the small, very pale green melons with orange flesh. They are rich in Vitamins A and C. Cut in half, remove seeds and scoop out the flesh. Steam for 3–5 minutes, then purée.

Other varieties of sweet melon, so long as they are ripe, can be used too. When your baby is over six months, properly ripe melon may be eaten raw.

MAKES 12–16 PORTIONS

Plum

Skin 2 large ripe plums as for peaches. Cut into pieces and bring to the boil in just enough water to cover. Simmer for about 5 minutes or until soft; add sugar or honey to taste if the fruit is a little sour. (Alternatively, steam for about 6 minutes.) Purée, adding as much of the cooking liquid as is necessary to make the purée the desired consistency.

Plums may be eaten raw once your baby is over six months.

MAKES 4 PORTIONS

Prune and Dried Apricot

Use 100 g/4 oz of fruit. Soak prunes in cold water overnight, then drain. Wash dried apricots well to remove preservative. Cover with fresh cold water, bring to the boil and simmer until soft (about 10 minutes). Drain, remove the stones and press through a mouli to remove the rough skins. Add a little of the cooking liquid to make a smooth purée.

Prunes are excellent if your baby gets constipated.

MAKES 4 PORTIONS

Apricots and Pears

Fresh apricots have a very limited season but when they are available you should make this delicious combination of fruits. Apricots are rich in Vitamins A and C. Halve and stone 5 fresh ripe apricots. Peel, core and slice 2 ripe pears. Steam the fruit until tender, about 6–8 minutes. When cool enough skin the apricots. Purée the fruit together in a mouli or blender.

MAKES 12 PORTIONS

Apple and Raisin Compote

Heat 3 tablespoons of fresh orange juice in a saucepan. Add 2 eating apples, peeled, cored and sliced and 15 g/½ oz of washed raisins. Cook gently for about 10 minutes until soft, adding a little water if necessary. Purée in a mouli to remove seeds and skins.

Dried fruit, even raisins, must always be put through a mouli for a baby.

MAKES 8 PORTIONS

Fresh Peas

Cover 100 g/4 oz podded peas with water, bring to the boil and simmer, covered, until tender (about 10 minutes). Drain, reserving some of the cooking liquid. Put the peas through a mouli or a sieve and add a little of the cooking liquid to make the purée the desired consistency.

MAKES 4 PORTIONS

Tomatoes

Plunge 2 medium tomatoes in boiling water for 30 seconds, then transfer to cold water. Skin, remove the seeds and cook the flesh in a heavy-bottomed saucepan, mashing over a low heat for about 2 minutes. Put through a mouli or sieve to purée.

MAKES 2–3 PORTIONS

Spinach

Wash 100 g/4 oz spinach leaves very carefully, removing the coarse stalks. Cover with boiling water and simmer, covered, until tender (about 10 minutes). Firmly press out all the excess cooking water and put the spinach leaves through a mouli to purée.

MAKES 2 PORTIONS

Celery

Wash 100 g/4 oz celery carefully, top and tail, and remove as many strings as possible. Cut into small pieces, cover with boiling water and simmer until tender (about 15 minutes). Drain and put the celery through a mouli.

Shredded cabbage can be cooked similarly but for about 10 minutes only.

MAKES 4 PORTIONS

Sweet Red Pepper

Wash a medium pepper, remove the core and seeds and cut the flesh into small cubes. Cover with boiling water and simmer, covered, for about 5 minutes. Drain and put through a mouli to get rid of the tough outer skin.

MAKES 2–3 PORTIONS

Avocado

Choose a well-ripened avocado, cut it in half and scoop out the stone. Use ⅓–½ and mash the flesh very carefully with a fork, making sure there are no lumps. Serve quickly, otherwise it will turn brown.

Do not freeze avocados.

MAKES 1 PORTION

Kiwi and Banana

Kiwi fruit are very good for your baby as they have more Vitamin C than an orange! Make sure you choose a very ripe fruit, otherwise it can be very sour.

MAKES 1 PORTION

¼ ripe kiwi, peeled   *¼ ripe banana, peeled*

Purée the kiwi and strain through a fine sieve to get rid of the black seeds. Purée the banana and mix it with the kiwi. Eat straight-away or the banana turns brown.

Apple and Banana with Orange Juice

This makes a nice change from plain mashed banana or apple purée. The recipe can be made with or without honey, depending on how sweet the fruit is. When your baby is six months or older, you can make this with raw grated apple and mashed banana.

MAKES 1 PORTION

¼ apple, peeled, cored and chopped   *½ teaspoon orange juice*
¼ banana, peeled and chopped   *¼ teaspoon honey (optional)*

Steam the apple until tender (about 10 minutes) then purée or mash it together with the banana, orange juice and honey (if used). Serve as soon as possible.

Peaches, Apples and Pears

This is a good purée to make when peaches are in season. When they are not it tastes good just with apples and pears.

MAKES 14 PORTIONS

2 eating apples, peeled, cored and chopped
1 cm/¹/₂ inch vanilla pod (optional)

2 ripe peaches, skinned and chopped
2 ripe pears, peeled, cored and chopped

Put the apple pieces in a saucepan with 50 ml/2 fl oz water and the vanilla pod. Simmer for about 5 minutes. Add the peaches and pears and cook for 5 minutes more. Remove the pod and purée.

Mixed Dried Fruit Compote

Dried fruits and fresh fruits are delicious combined. Later on mix with a little natural yoghurt or fromage frais.

MAKES 18 PORTIONS

50 g/2 oz each of dried apricots, dried peaches and prunes

1 eating apple and pear, peeled, cored and chopped or 1 apple and 3 fresh apricots, skinned, stoned and chopped

Put the dried fruit into a saucepan, cover with plenty of boiling water and simmer for 25 minutes until tender. Add the apple and pear or apricots to the saucepan. Continue to simmer for another 10–15 minutes, adding more water if necessary. Purée in a mouli.

Vegetable Stock

Vegetable stock forms the basis of many vegetable recipes. It is well worth making your own supply which will be free from additives and salt. Freeze it as you would any other stock.

MAKES ABOUT 900 ml/1½ PINTS

½ onion, peeled
1 carrot, scrubbed
1 celery stalk
175 g/6 oz mixed root vegetables
(swede, turnip, parsnip, etc), peeled

1 bouquet garni (bought or home-made)
1 sprig of fresh parsley
1 bay leaf
a few black peppercorns

Chop all the vegetables, place in a pan and cover with water. Add the seasonings, bring to the boil and simmer for about 1 hour. Strain off and discard the vegetables and use the flavoured water as stock.

Courgette and Banana Purée

This may seem a strange combination but they complement each other well.

MAKES 2 PORTIONS

1 small courgette, washed, trimmed and sliced

½ small banana, peeled and sliced

Steam the courgette slices for 8 minutes and purée in a mouli with the banana.

Baby Cereal and Vegetables

Sometimes vegetable purées can be very watery – particularly those made from, say, courgettes which have a high water content. In this recipe I have added baby rice which makes an excellent thickening agent.

MAKES 16 PORTIONS

¼ small onion, peeled
2 courgettes, trimmed
50 g/2 oz broccoli, cut into florets
2 medium carrots, peeled

25 g/1 oz green cabbage, shredded
25 g/1 oz fresh peas
vegetable stock (see page 33)
3 tablespoons baby rice

Chop all the vegetables, put them in a saucepan and just cover them with the stock. Bring to the boil, then simmer for 30 minutes or until the vegetables are tender. Add the baby cereal and stir over a gentle heat for 2 minutes. Purée the vegetables in a blender until the desired consistency.

Vegetable Medley

This is a good combination of fresh vegetables. Steamed beans, cauliflower and courgettes also make great finger foods for slightly older babies. Do not steam the vegetables too long or they will become mushy and lose Vitamin C.

MAKES 10 PORTIONS

50 g/2 oz green beans, topped, tailed and sliced
50 g/2 oz cauliflower, cut into small florets

50 g/2 oz courgettes, trimmed and sliced
1 medium tomato (about 50 g/2 oz), skinned, seeded and chopped

Steam the beans, cauliflower and courgettes for about 6–7 minutes. Add the tomato to the steamer and continue to cook until all the vegetables are tender (about another 4 minutes). Purée and sieve the vegetables or put them through a mouli.

Courgette, Watercress and Potato Purée

Watercress is rich in calcium and iron. It blends well with the other vegetables to make a tasty, bright green purée. You can add a little milk if your baby prefers it that way.

MAKES 12 PORTIONS

a handful of watercress
1 large potato, peeled and chopped
350 ml/12 fl oz vegetable stock (see page 33)

1 dessertspoon chopped parsley
75 g/3 oz courgettes
washed, trimmed and sliced
baby milk (optional)

Remove the leaves from the watercress and chop them into pieces. (Discard the stalks, or use them in making vegetable stock.) Put the leaves and the potato into the stock, bring to the boil and simmer for about 10 minutes. Add the parsley and courgette and simmer for another 10 minutes. Purée the mixture in a mouli and, if you like, add a little baby milk to adjust the consistency.

Avocado and Papaya

This is very simple to make and the two fruits blend very well.

MAKES 1 PORTION

¹/₄ small avacado   *¹/₄ small papaya*

Remove the flesh from the avocado and papaya and mash them together until smooth. This should be eaten soon after it is made or the avocado will turn brown.

Sweet Potato with Cinnamon

The addition of cinnamon gives the sweet potato an extra sweetness which babies love. This is very simple to make.

MAKES 7 PORTIONS

1 sweet potato (about 6 oz/175 g),   *1 tablespoon baby milk*
peeled and cut into chunks   *¹/₄ teaspoon powdered cinnamon*

Cover the sweet potato chunks with water, bring to the boil and simmer for about 30 minutes or until soft. Drain and mash together with the baby milk and cinnamon.

Leek Quartet

Often forgotten, leeks have a wonderful flavour and combine with many different vegetables to make delicious purées.

MAKES 13 PORTIONS

1 medium potato, peeled and chopped
50 g/2 oz white of leek, carefully washed, trimmed and chopped
1 large tomato, skinned, seeded and chopped

1 small carrot, peeled and chopped
250 ml/8 fl oz vegetable stock (see page 33)
1 tablespoon chopped parsley

Simmer all the vegetables in the stock for about 20 minutes. Add the parsley and put the mixture through a mouli.

Baked Butternut Squash

The flavour of butternut squash is delicious simply baked with a little orange juice, margarine and brown sugar. You can also scoop out the seeds and stuff the squash with vegetables as in this recipe.

MAKES 6 PORTIONS

1 small butternut squash
1 teaspoon brown sugar
1 tablespoon orange juice

½ oz/15 g margarine
1 small courgette, diced
1 tomato, skinned, seeded and diced

Cut the squash in half lengthwise and scoop out the seeds. Mix the rest of the ingredients together and divide between the two cavities. Cover both halves with foil and bake in the oven preheated to 350°F(180°C)Gas 4 for 1½ hours. Scoop the flesh out of the skin and mash or purée with the vegetable filling.

FOUR TO FIVE MONTH MEAL PLANNER

Week 1	Breakfast	Sleep	Lunch	Sleep	Tea	Bedtime
Days 1–7	Breast/bottle	Breast/bottle	Breast/bottle Baby rice	Breast/bottle	Diluted fruit juice	Breast/bottle
Week 2						
Day 1	Breast/bottle Baby rice	Breast/bottle	Breast/bottle	Breast/bottle	Diluted fruit juice Carrot	Breast/bottle
Day 2	Breast/bottle Baby rice	Breast/bottle	Breast/bottle	Breast/bottle	Diluted fruit juice Carrot	Breast/bottle
Day 3	Breast/bottle Baby rice Apple	Breast/bottle	Breast/bottle	Breast/bottle	Diluted fruit juice Carrot	Breast/bottle
Day 4	Breast/bottle Apple	Breast/bottle	Breast/bottle	Breast/bottle	Diluted fruit juice Swede	Breast/bottle
Day 5	Breast/bottle Apple	Breast/bottle	Breast/bottle	Breast/bottle	Diluted fruit juice Swede	Breast/bottle
Day 6	Breast/bottle Baby rice Pear	Breast/bottle	Breast/bottle	Breast/bottle	Diluted fruit juice Potato	Breast/bottle
Day 7	Breast/bottle Pear	Breast/bottle	Breast/bottle	Breast/bottle	Diluted fruit juice Potato	Breast/bottle

Fruit juice should be diluted at least 50/50 with cooled boiled water.

FOUR TO FIVE MONTH MEAL PLANNER

Week 3	Breakfast	Sleep	Lunch	Sleep	Tea	Bedtime
Day 1	Breast/bottle Mashed banana	Breast/bottle	Breast/bottle	Breast/bottle	Fruit juice or herbal tea Potato and green beans	Breast/bottle
Day 2	Breast/bottle Mashed banana	Breast/bottle	Breast/bottle	Breast/bottle	Fruit juice or herbal tea Potato and green beans	Breast/bottle
Day 3	Breast/bottle Cream of Fruit	Breast/bottle	Breast/bottle	Breast/bottle	Diluted fruit juice Butternut squash	Breast/bottle
Day 4	Breast/bottle Cream of Fruit	Breast/bottle	Breast/bottle	Breast/bottle	Diluted fruit juice Butternut squash	Breast/bottle
Day 5	Breast/bottle Banana Papaya	Breast/bottle	Breast/bottle	Breast/bottle	Green beans Baby rice	Breast/bottle
Day 6	Breast/bottle Pear	Breast/bottle	Breast/bottle	Breast/bottle	Green beans Baby rice	Breast/bottle
Day 7	Breast/bottle Pear	Breast/bottle	Breast/bottle	Breast/bottle	Carrot and Cauliflower Purée	Breast/bottle

Fruit juice should be diluted at least 50/50 with cooled boiled water.

FOUR TO FIVE MONTH MEAL PLANNER

Week 4	Breakfast	Sleep	Lunch	Sleep	Tea	Bedtime
Day 1	Breast/bottle Cream of Fruit	Breast/bottle	Breast/bottle	Breast/bottle	Fruit juice Cream of Carrot Purée	Breast/bottle
Day 2	Breast/bottle Cream of Fruit	Breast/bottle	Breast/bottle	Breast/bottle	Fruit juice Cream of Carrot Purée	Breast/bottle
Day 3	Breast/bottle Three Fruit Purée	Breast/bottle	Breast/bottle	Breast/bottle	Fruit juice Potato, Courgette and Green Beans	Breast/bottle
Day 4	Breast/bottle Three Fruit Purée	Breast/bottle	Breast/bottle	Breast/bottle	Fruit juice Potato, Courgette and Green Beans	Breast/bottle
Day 5	Breast/bottle mashed banana	Breast/bottle	Breast/bottle	Breast/bottle	Fruit juice Broccoli Trio	Breast/bottle
Day 6	Breast/bottle Apples and Cinnamon	Breast/bottle	Breast/bottle	Breast/bottle	Fruit juice Broccoli Trio	Breast/bottle
Day 7	Breast/bottle Apples and Cinnamon	Breast/bottle	Breast/bottle	Breast/bottle	Fruit juice Swede	Breast/bottle

Fruit juice should be diluted at least 50/50 with cooled boiled water.

FIVE TO SIX MONTH MEAL PLANNER

	Breakfast	Sleep	Lunch	Sleep	Tea	Bedtime
Day 1	Milk Baby cereal mixed fruit purée and milk	Milk	Leek Quartet Juice	Milk	Mashed banana Rusk Water or juice	Milk
Day 2	Milk Rusk Apple and Raisin Compote	Milk	Avocado Juice	Milk	Mixed Dried Fruit Compote Water or juice	Milk
Day 3	Milk Baby cereal Peach or pear	Milk	Sweet Potato with Cinnamon Juice	Milk	Cream of Fruit Water or juice	Milk
Day 4	Milk Dried apricot Yoghurt	Milk	Baby Cereal and Vegetables Juice	Milk	Papaya Rusk Water or juice	Milk
Day 5	Milk Baby cereal Papaya	Milk	Baked Butter-nut Squash Mashed banana Juice	Milk	Avocado and Papaya Rice cake Water or juice	Milk
Day 6	Milk Baby cereal Apple and Cinnamon	Milk	Potato, Courgette and Green Beans Juice	Milk	Three-Fruit Purée Rusk Water or juice	Milk
Day 7	Milk Mixed Dried Fruit Compote Yoghurt	Milk	Courgette, Watercress and Potato Purée Juice	Milk	Mashed banana Rice cake Water or juice	Milk

Fruit juice should be diluted at least 50/50 with cooled boiled water.

CHAPTER THREE

SIX TO NINE MONTHS

Between six and nine months is a rapid development period for your baby. A six-month old baby still needs to be held whilst you are feeding him and more often than not, still has no teeth. A nine-month old baby, however, is usually strong enough to sit in a high chair whilst he is being fed and has already cut a few teeth. Babies of eight months are usually quite good at holding food themselves and enjoy eating small finger foods like pieces of raw or cooked vegetables, pasta or raw fruits. (Turn to pages 72–78 for suitable finger foods for young babies.) Chewing on a piece of apple will help to relieve sore gums but *never* leave your baby unattended when eating; babies have a habit of chewing up a lot of food and storing it in their mouths without swallowing and they can very easily choke. A handy tip is to give your baby some dried apple to suck; it is easy for them to hold because of the hole in the middle; it is tough to chew on so they cannot bite pieces off; and it has a lovely sweet taste.

Less Milk, More Appetite

Once your baby is six months old, you can start cutting down on his milk feeds so that he is more hungry for his solids. However he should still be taking about 600 ml/1 pint of milk per day, either as milk or in dairy products he eats. You can offer plain water or fruit juices or low-sugar herbal drinks instead of milk.

At eight or nine months, when your baby holds toys fairly well himself, he is probably ready to try drinking from a cup. First try a cup with a spout then remove the top and see how he manages with it open. A cup with a weighted base is good so that it does not topple over and spill when your baby puts it down.

Let your baby's appetite determine how much he eats and never force him to eat something he actually dislikes. Do not offer it for a while, but re-introduce it a few weeks later. You may find that second time around he loves it.

Remember at this age it is quite normal for babies to be quite fat. As soon as your baby starts crawling and walking, he will lose this excess weight.

The Foods to Choose

Your baby can now eat protein foods like eggs, cheese, pulses, chicken and, after eight months, fish. Limit some foods which might be indigestible – spinach, lentils, cheese, berry or citrus fruit and do not worry if some foods like pulses, peas and raisins pass through your child undigested; babies cannot completely digest husked vegetables and the skins of fruits until about two years old. Peeling, mashing and puréeing fruit and vegetables will of course aid digestion. With foods like bread, flour, pasta and rice, try to choose whole-grain (rather than refined) as it is more nutritious.

Once your baby has passed the six-month stage and is happily eating bread and other foods containing gluten, there is no need to continue giving your baby special baby cereals. You can use adult cereals like Ready Brek, instant porridge and Weetabix which are just as nutritious and much cheaper. Choose a cereal which is not highly refined and is low in sugar and salt. Many people use commercial baby foods because they are easy to prepare; they also think, due to the long list of vitamins and minerals on the packet, that they are more nutritious. However, babies who eat a good balanced diet of fresh foods get a perfectly adequate quantity of vitamins and minerals. Also baby foods in general are heavily processed and their finer texture and bland flavours hinder development of your baby's tastes.

Beware, too, of some of the rusks you can buy which are supposedly the 'ideal food for your baby'. They are full of sugar (the amount often not even stated on the list of ingredients). Give your baby some toast to chew on or follow the simple recipe for rusks in the nine to twelve month finger-food section (see page 77).

Many of your own favourite recipes can be adapted for your baby once he is eight months old. When preparing a family dish, put aside the baby's portion before you add seasoning or spices and he can very often enjoy the same meal as everyone else. Many of the recipes from the previous age group's section can still be used – simply alter the texture slightly if appropriate and offer more.

You can now safely cook with cow's milk. This is not suitable for milk feeds (formula or breast is better).

FRUIT

There are few babies I know who do not like fruit. In the next few months, try to introduce your child to as wide a range of fruits as possible. Make fresh fruit salads with seasonal fruits chopped into little pieces and mixed with orange juice. You will find which fruits your child likes best by seeing what he leaves.

Citrus fruits, berries, dried fruits and some exotic fruits like mango can give your child an upset stomach. Limit these or you may run out of nappies! Try to remove all pith from citrus fruits to make them easier to digest.

Fresh fruit makes excellent snacks – much better than processed, additive-laden, sugary foods which ruin developing teeth and upset a balanced diet.

VEGETABLES

Once your baby starts to get teeth, you will find that he enjoys chewing on slightly harder vegetables. Cut down the steaming time to preserve Vitamin C and keep them crisp. Cauliflower and broccoli florets, baby carrots and baby sweetcorn, for instance – make excellent finger foods. Give them to your baby with his favourite vegetable purée as a dip.

Remember that some vegetables such as new potatoes and courgettes should not be peeled to preserve nutrients in the skin. Combinations of fruit and vegetables are popular – try squash and apple; spinach and pear or devise your own.

FISH

Many children grow up disliking fish, which is a great shame as it is such a healthy food, full of protein and very low in fat. It is excellent for babies, easy to chew and digest and quick to cook.

I think one of the main reasons children are put off fish is that they find it bland and boring. Counteract this with stronger tastes like cheese or tomato. If your child gets excited at the prospect of fish for dinner, then you deserve to be a very proud mum indeed.

Most paediatricians advise against fish before eight months. Start with white fish only and give oily fish after 10–12 months.

Be careful not to overcook fish, as it becomes tough and tasteless. It is cooked when the fish just flakes with a fork but is still firm. Always check very carefully for bones before serving fish.

MEAT

Chicken is the first meat that should be introduced to babies. Chicken is a great family favourite of ours; it is very versatile and I am always concocting new ways of serving it. I was keen to get Nicholas and Lara to like chicken from an early age so I could cook for the whole family.

I have found that babies like the mild taste of chicken. It is easy and quick to cook; a great help to busy mothers. Chicken blends very well with many vegetables and can have a smooth texture when puréed. Once your baby is able to handle food himself and has a few teeth, small pieces of chicken make excellent finger food and are softer and easier to chew than red meat chunks.

Home-made chicken stock forms the basis of many recipes and I recommend that you make it in large batches. Freeze in small containers or ice-cube trays.

PASTA

You will find that pasta is a great favourite with babies and mums as it is easy to chew, fun to eat and easy to cook.

For babies around six months, there are very tiny pasta shapes available which are sometimes used in soups and need no chewing or you could chop up spaghetti. Many of the vegetable purées make excellent pasta sauces, and you can always add a little grated cheese. Serve about 25 g/ 1 oz cooked (10–15 g/¼–½ oz dry) pasta per portion.

Textures

For babies between six and eight months, the recipes should be puréed to a fairly smooth consistency. Thereafter the mixture can be coarser, with the foods mashed, finely chopped or grated or make a gradual transition by adding grated food to a purée. Foods must be soft enough for the toothless gums to chew.

Quantities

The portions quoted for each recipe are still ice-cube-tray size. Babies at this stage can eat between 1 and 4 tablespoons at each meal. On average thaw 4 frozen food-cubes, two of a savoury food and two of a fruit purée.

FRUIT

Baked Bananas

Babies love bananas and this recipe makes them taste truly scrumptious. You can make this recipe Jamaican style by using brown sugar instead of maple syrup and adding the juice of one orange. It can also be cooked in a frying pan and flambéed with rum for a dinner party. Serve with vanilla ice cream.

MAKES 1 PORTION

1 banana, sliced in half lengthwise
1 teaspoon maple syrup

powdered cinnamon
margarine or butter

Put the banana into an ovenproof dish. Pour over the maple syrup, sprinkle with a little cinnamon and dot with a little margarine or butter. Cover with foil and bake at 350°F (180°C) Gas 4 for 10 minutes.

Avocado, Banana and Yoghurt

This should be eaten straightaway before it turns brown.

MAKES 1 PORTION

2 slices avocado,
½ small banana, peeled

1 tablespoon natural Greek yoghurt

Scoop the flesh of the avocado from the skin and mash it together with the rest of the ingredients.

Apple and Baby Cereal

Try using different fruits such as peaches, mangoes, plums and combinations like apple and raisin, and peach and redcurrant.

MAKES 6 PORTIONS

1 eating apple, peeled, cored and cut into small pieces
85 ml/3 fl oz natural apple juice

2 teaspoons baby cereal
2 teaspoons natural yoghurt

Cook the apple over a low heat with the apple juice and 2 tablespoons water until soft (about 15 minutes). Purée the apple with the cooking liquid, then stir in the cereal and yoghurt.

Peaches and Rice

You could use nectarines or plums or add raisins and spices.

MAKES 10 PORTIONS

50 g/2 oz brown rice
apple juice

2 ripe peaches, skinned and stoned
natural yoghurt or fromage frais

Cover rice with apple juice and cook 20 minutes or until tender. Purée the peaches, mix with the rice and bake in a buttered dish for 15–20 minutes at 350°F(180°C)Gas 4. Purée in a blender and serve plain or mixed with a little fromage frais or yoghurt.

Apple and Prunes with Custard

Babies should not eat eggs before eight months but this eggless custard always goes down well poured over, or stirred into, fruit.

MAKES 20 PORTIONS

8 prunes, soaked overnight
4 apples

Eggless custard
200 ml/7 fl oz milk
1 tablespoon custard powder
1 teaspoon caster sugar

Simmer the prunes gently in the soaking water till tender (about 10 minutes). Meanwhile make an apple purée (see page 24). Stone, then purée the prunes in a mouli. Mix together with the apple purée.

To make the custard, put 175 ml/6 fl oz milk in a saucepan and bring to the boil. Stir the custard powder and sugar into the remaining cold milk and stir until smooth. Stir this into the hot milk off the heat. Bring to the boil and stir until thickened.

Cottage Cheese and Sharon Fruit

Sharon fruit looks like an orange tomato. It must be very ripe and soft before it is eaten, and tastes a little like a sweet plum. The second portion will keep in the fridge for the next day.

MAKES 2 PORTIONS

1 Sharon fruit, or 2 slices of mango
or papaya

2 tablespoons plain cottage cheese

Cut the Sharon fruit in half and remove the skin. Blend the flesh together with the cottage cheese until smooth.

Home-Made Fruit Jelly

It is very easy to make fruit jelly at home and it is not full of sugar or artificial colourings like some of the commercially prepared fruit jellies. If you are short of time or don't have fresh fruit purées or juices to hand, packet jelly can be used for any of these recipes. Jelly, of course, does not freeze but any extras have never been a problem in my house!

MAKES 12 PORTIONS

1 envelope of powdered gelatine   *600 ml/1 pint fresh fruit juice or fruit purée*

Sprinkle the gelatine over 50 ml/2 fl oz warmed fruit juice (or water if using fruit purée) in a cup. Stand the cup in a pan of hot water if necessary until gelatine dissolves. Pour into the remaining fruit juice or purée, stirring thoroughly. Pour into a suitable container, cool, then chill until set.

Fruit Jelly Shapes Set jelly in a 20 cm/8 inch square tin, lined with foil. Turn the tin over, remove the foil and make different shapes from the jelly using biscuit cutters.

Fruit and Yoghurt Jelly Make up ½ quantity of any fruit flavoured jelly and chill for 30 minutes, then stir in a complementary flavoured fruit yoghurt. Chill again to set. This jelly will not set firm and so is not suitable for a mould.

Traffic Light Jelly Make up a ½ quantity of jelly using a green coloured fruit juice or purée. Pour into a large fluted jelly mould. (A wet mould makes it easier to turn the jelly out.) Chill for 1½ hours. Repeat with an orange coloured juice or purée and pour on top. Chill again and then add a layer of a red jelly. Chill until set. Dip into hot water, cover with a plate and then turn over to unmould.

VEGETABLES

Lentil Purée

Lentils are usually soaked overnight but you can take a shortcut. Rinse them, cover generously with the stock, bring to the boil and boil for 2 minutes. Take off the heat, cover the pan and let the lentils absorb the stock for 1–2 hours.
Lentils are a good cheap source of protein but are best not given to babies before eight months.

MAKES 36 PORTIONS

50 g/2 oz split red lentils
600 ml/1 pint chicken stock
(preferably home-made, see page 62)
1 carrot

1 potato
½ small onion
½ white of leek
15 g/½ oz margarine or 1 tablespoon oil

S oak the lentils overnight in the stock. The next day, peel and dice the carrot, potato and onion and shred the washed leek. Sauté the onion and leek in the margarine or oil until soft, then add the carrot and potato and continue to cook for a further 5 minutes. Add the lentils and stock, bring to the boil, then simmer for about 40 minutes or until the lentils are soft. Purée if wished.

Tomatoes with Fennel and Basil

If you introduce your baby to new flavours at an early age, he will tend to grow up a less fussy eater. Fennel has an interesting flavour and blends well with the tomato in this recipe.

MAKES 12 PORTIONS

1 medium potato, about 175 g/6 oz
1 large tomato
¼ small fennel bulb, about 50 g/2 oz

1 dessertspoon chopped fresh basil
15 g/½ oz margarine or 1 tablespoon oil

Peel and trim the vegetables, removing skin and seeds from the tomato. Cut into pieces and cook the potato and fennel in water to cover over a low heat for 15 minutes. Meanwhile sauté the tomato and chopped basil in the margarine for 2–3 minutes until they turn into a purée. Press everything through a mouli.

French Beans with Tomato and Apple

The apple brings out the sweet taste of the beans and tomato. This purée is very good mixed with cottage cheese.

MAKES 10 PORTIONS

75 g/3 oz French beans
1 apple, peeled, cored and chopped

1 medium tomato, skinned, seeded and chopped

String the beans then wash them carefully. Steam with the apple for about 10 minutes or until tender. After 6 minutes add the tomato. Process in a blender until the desired consistency.

Special Spinach and Potato Purée

This purée makes a tasty introduction to spinach for your baby. It also makes a nice vegetable side dish for adults.

MAKES 14 PORTIONS

1 onion, peeled and finely chopped
25 g/1 oz margarine
8 oz/225 g spinach, washed, chopped and tough stalks removed

1 large or 2 small potatoes, peeled and diced
120 ml/4 fl oz chicken stock (see page 62)

Sauté the onion in the margarine over a low heat for 4–5 minutes until soft. Add the spinach and potato, pour in the stock and simmer slowly for about 35 minutes. Purée in a blender.

Oat and Vegetable Purée

Oats add bulk to the vegetable purée making it a satisfying meal.

MAKES 20 PORTIONS

1 celery stalk
1 white part of leek, washed carefully
2 medium or 4 small carrots
50 g/2 oz each of mushrooms, swede,

cauliflower and broccoli
3 tablespoons porridge oats
1 tablespoon chopped parsley

Peel, trim as appropriate and finely chop all the vegetables. Just cover the vegetables with water in a saucepan and add the porridge oats. Bring the water to the boil, then cover and simmer for about 20 minutes or until the vegetables are tender. Purée in a blender until the desired consistency. Mix in the chopped parsley.

Trio of Cauliflower, Red Sweet Pepper and Sweetcorn

If you want to freeze a dish containing sweetcorn, you should use either fresh or canned sweetcorn in your recipe – frozen sweetcorn should not be re-frozen. Always purée sweetcorn in a mouli for young babies to get rid of the tough outer skin.

MAKES 10 PORTIONS

100 g/4 oz cauliflower, cut into small florets
120 ml/4 fl oz milk

25 g/1 oz chopped red sweet pepper
75 g/3 oz sweetcorn

Put the cauliflower in a saucepan with the milk and cook over a low heat for about 12 minutes until tender. Meanwhile, cook the red pepper and sweetcorn in water in a saucepan for about 6 minutes until tender.

Drain the sweetcorn and pepper. Purée together with the cauliflower and milk in a mouli.

Cauliflower Cheese

This is a great favourite with babies. Try using different cheeses or combinations of cheese until you find your baby's favourite taste. Try using the cheese sauce over a mixture of vegetables as well.

MAKES 15 PORTIONS

175 g/6 oz cauliflower

Cheese sauce
15 g/½ oz margarine
1 tablespoon cornflour
175 ml/6 fl oz milk
50 g/2 oz grated Cheddar, Edam or Gruyère cheese

Wash the cauliflower carefully, divide it into small florets and steam until tender (about 10 minutes). Meanwhile, for the sauce, melt the margarine over a gentle heat in a heavy-bottomed saucepan and stir in the cornflour to make a smooth paste. Add the milk and stir until thickened. Take the saucepan off the heat and stir in the grated cheese. Keep stirring until all the cheese has melted and the sauce is smooth.

Add the cauliflower to the sauce and purée in a blender for younger babies. For older babies, mash with a fork or chop into little pieces.

Courgette Gratin

This creamy purée is also good using green beans or broccoli.

MAKES 18 PORTIONS

1 medium potato, about 100 g/4 oz, peeled
175 g/6 oz courgettes, sliced
120 ml/4 fl oz milk

25 g/1 oz Gruyère or Emmenthal cheese, grated
1 sprig of parsley, chopped
a little margarine

Boil the potato until soft, then drain. Steam the courgettes for 8 minutes. Purée all together in a mouli or blender.

Leek and Potato Purée with Fromage Frais

This is Lara's favourite vegetable purée. It also makes a superb vegetable soup for adults.

MAKES 16 PORTIONS

25 g/1 oz margarine or 2 tablespoons oil
175 g/6 oz leeks, carefully washed and sliced

225 g/8 oz potatoes, peeled and diced
450 ml/15 fl oz chicken stock (see page 62)
2 tablespoons fromage frais

Heat the margarine in a heavy-based pan. Add the leeks and cook over a gentle heat for 10 minutes until softened, stirring occasionally. Add the diced potatoes and stock and simmer, covered, for 25–30 minutes until tender. Purée and stir in the fromage frais.

Tasty Lettuce and Courgette Purée

When I experimented with this combination, the baby purée that I
made turned out to be so good that I increased the quantities and
made a delicious soup for the whole family. It is very healthy and
low in calories too!

MAKES 4 PORTIONS

½ onion, peeled and finely chopped
15 g/1½ oz margarine or 1 tablespoon
oil
50 g/2 oz courgette, washed, trimmed
and thinly sliced

100 g/4 oz iceberg lettuce, shredded
50 ml/2 fl oz good chicken stock (see
page 62)

Sauté the onion in the margarine over a low heat for about 3
minutes until soft. Add the courgette and lettuce and continue to
cook over a low heat for 3 minutes. Pour over the chicken stock and
cook, covered, for a further 3 minutes.

Purée in a blender until the
desired consistency for your
baby. As a soup for the whole
family, I think it is better if it is
not too smooth. ☺ ☹

Minestrone

This is a very versatile recipe, as you can add rice, pasta or almost any vegetable. I find the flavour is best if you use chicken stock.

MAKES 7 ADULT PORTIONS OR 40 BABY PORTIONS

15 g/¹/₂ oz margarine or 1 tablespoon oil
¹/₂ small onion, peeled and chopped
1 carrot, peeled and chopped
¹/₂ celery stalk, chopped
¹/₂ white of leek, chopped
100 g/4 oz cabbage, shredded
1.2 litres/2 pints water, chicken or vegetable stock (see pages 62 and 33)

1 potato, about 100 g/4 oz, peeled and diced
3 tablespoons podded peas
1 tablespoon chopped parsley
2 teaspoons tomato paste
50 g/2 oz small pasta shapes (optional)

Heat the margarine in a saucepan and fry the onion for 1 minute, then add the carrot, celery and leek. Sauté these for 2 minutes, then add the cabbage and continue to cook for another 4 minutes.

Cover with the water or stock. Add the potato, peas, chopped parsley and tomato paste and cook over a gentle heat for 20–25 minutes until the vegetables are soft and easy for your baby to chew (for younger babies, you can mash or purée the vegetables). If you want pasta in the soup, then add this 10 minutes prior to the end of cooking.

FISH

Plaice with Tomatoes and Potato

This makes a good, creamy-textured fish purée.

MAKES 4 PORTIONS

1 fillet of plaice, skinned
2 medium tomatoes, skinned, seeded
and chopped

a little margarine or butter
1 bay leaf
150 ml/5 fl oz milk
1 small potato, peeled

Put the plaice into a dish, cover with the chopped tomato, dot with a little margarine and add the bay leaf. Pour over most of the milk. Cover with foil and cook in the oven preheated to 350°F(180°C)Gas 4, for 20 minutes. (Alternatively cover with a lid and cook in the microwave on High for about 3 minutes.)

Whilst the fish is cooking, boil the potato. When soft, mash it with the remaining milk and margarine. Flake the fish when it is cooked, remove the bay leaf and purée the fish together with the liquid in which it was cooked. You can either mix in the mashed potato or serve it as an accompaniment to the fish.

Plaice in Cheese Sauce

Fish and cheese sauce go really well together and the combination
is always popular. Add some chives and you give an old recipe a
new taste.

MAKES 8 PORTIONS

1 plaice, filleted and skinned
120 ml/4 fl oz milk
1 sprig of parsley
1 small tomato, quartered
a few mushrooms or mushroom stalks

Cheese sauce
25 g/1 oz margarine
25 g/1 oz plain flour
120 ml/4 fl oz milk
75 g/3 oz Cheddar cheese, grated
*1 teaspoon snipped chives or chopped
parsley*

Put the plaice fillets in an ovenproof dish, pour the milk over and
surround the fish with the parsley, tomato and mushrooms. Cover
with aluminium foil and cook in an oven preheated to
350°F(180°C)Gas 4 for about 20 minutes, or until the fish just flakes
with a fork. Strain the milk, discarding the vegetables.

When the fish is cooked, prepare the sauce. Melt the margarine in a
small saucepan and stir in the flour. Cook for 1 minute then stir in the
milk and fish cooking liquid gradually until you have a smooth white
sauce. Take the saucepan off the heat and stir in the cheese. When all
the cheese has melted, add the snipped chives or parsley.

Flake the fish with a fork and make sure there are no stray bones.
Add the fish to the cheese sauce and put it through the mouli to make
it into a smooth purée for your baby.

Plaice with Spinach and Cheese

This makes a very tasty dark green fish purée. You could use
Gruyère cheese instead.

MAKES 8 PORTIONS

1 plaice, filleted and skinned
1 tablespoon milk
1 bay leaf
a little margarine

100 g/4 oz spinach, washed and
tough stalks removed
100 g/4 oz Cheddar cheese, grated

Cook the plaice with the milk, bay leaf and margarine as in the
previous recipe. Meanwhile cook the spinach in boiling water
(about 10 minutes), then drain well and squeeze out any excess water.
Discard the bay leaf and put all the remaining ingredients in a food
processor, blend for about 1 minute and serve as a purée.

Fillet of Cod with Courgette

Cooking fish and vegetables wrapped in foil in the oven is a good
way of sealing in the natural flavour. Cutlets of fish (on the bone)
are also very good cooked this way. Experiment using a variety of
different vegetables.

MAKES 3 PORTIONS

1 medium courgette, washed and
trimmed
75 g/3 oz fillet of cod, skinned

1 sprig of fresh thyme
juice of ¹/₂ lemon
1 dessertspoon olive oil

Cut the courgette into small strips. Lay the fish on a piece of aluminium foil together with the courgette and thyme, sprinkle with lemon juice and olive oil and fold up into a parcel. Cook in an oven preheated to 350°F(180°C)Gas 4 for about 20 minutes. Before serving, flake the fish with a fork. Make sure there are no bones and remove the thyme.

Haddock in an Orange Sauce

This is one of my family's favourite fish recipes. Do not be put off by the odd combination it gives a marvellous rich taste.

MAKES 5 PORTIONS

225 g/8 oz fillet of haddock, skinned
juice of 1 orange
40 g/1½ oz Cheddar cheese, grated
1 dessertspoon finely chopped parsley

1 tomato, skinned, seeded and
chopped
25 g/1 oz crushed cornflakes
7 g/¼ oz margarine

Put the haddock in a greased dish, cover with the orange juice, cheese, parsley, tomato and cornflakes and dot with the margarine. Cover with foil and bake at 350°F(180°C)Gas 4 for about 20 minutes.

Flake the fish carefully, removing any bones and mash everything together with the liquid in which the fish was cooked.

CHICKEN

Chicken Stock and My First Chicken Purée

Recipes taste much better if you use home-made chicken stock rather than a stock cube. I make it in large batches, divide it up into small containers, keep it in the freezer and use it as a base for soups, and chicken and vegetable purées.

MAKES APPROXIMATELY 2.25 LITRES/4 PINTS

1 boiler chicken, plus giblets
2 parsnips
1 small turnip
3 carrots

2 leeks
2 large onions
1 celery stalk
3 sprigs of parsley

Cut the chicken into eight pieces, trimming excess fat. Trim, peel and wash the vegetables as necessary. Put the chicken pieces into a large saucepan together with the giblets. Cover generously with water, bring to the boil and skim the froth from the top. Add the vegetables and parsley and simmer for about 3½ hours. It is best to remove the chicken breasts after about 1½ hours if you are going to eat them, otherwise they will become too dry.)

Leave the soup in the fridge overnight and remove any congealed fat from the top in the morning. Strain out all the chicken and vegetables to make the chicken stock. Season to taste.

You can purée some of the chicken breast in a mouli together with a selection of the vegetables and some stock to make a chicken and vegetable purée for your baby, or purée the vegetables and stock for a non-clear soup for adults!

Chicken with Cottage Cheese

Babies of this age are a little too young to eat pieces of chicken as finger food. This and the following two recipes show you simple ways of transforming cold chicken into tasty food for your baby.

MAKES 6 PORTIONS

50 g/2 oz cooked boneless chicken, chopped
1 tablespoon natural yoghurt

1¹/₂ tablespoons cottage cheese with pineappple

Mix together the chicken, yoghurt and cottage cheese. Put through a mouli to make a smooth purée.

Chicken with Rice and Beans

MAKES 10 PORTIONS

75 g/3 oz green beans
50 g/2 oz brown rice
3 tablespoons apple juice

50 g/2 oz cooked boneless chicken, chopped

Steam the beans until tender and cook the rice in water (about 20 minutes). Mix all the ingredients together and blend in a food processor. Put through a mouli to make a smooth purée. (You can add more apple juice if it is too thick.)

Chicken with Potato and Tomatoes

MAKES 6 PORTIONS

1 medium potato, peeled
2 tablespoons milk
1 medium tomato, skinned,
seeded

50 g/2 oz cooked boneless chicken,
chopped

Boil the potato until soft. Mash the potato with the milk and the tomato flesh, then add the chicken. Make into a purée in the blender. (If too thick, add a little extra milk.)

Chicken Salad Purée

What could be simpler. For toddlers, chop the ingredients and mix with mayonnaise or salad cream.

MAKES 4 PORTIONS

25 g/1 oz cooked boneless chicken,
chopped
1 chunk of cucumber
1 small tomato, skinned and seeded
1 dessertspoon natural yoghurt or
cottage cheese

1 teaspoon chopped chives
1 slice avocado

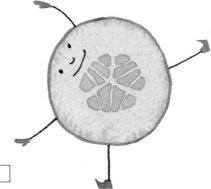

Put all the ingredients into a blender and purée until the desired consistency.

Chicken and Peach Delight

This is a delicious combination; it's very simple to make and popular with young children of all ages.

MAKES 10 PORTIONS

*50 g/2 oz cooked boneless chicken,
chopped
50 g/2 oz cooked brown rice
1 ripe peach*

*1 tablespoon peach juice
1 tablespoon milk
1 dessertspoon wheatgerm*

Just mix all the ingredients together and chop roughly in the food processor.

☺ ☹

Chicken and Mixed Vegetable Purée

This purée makes a very tasty introduction to chicken for your baby. Made in larger quantities, and seasoned after the baby's portions have been removed to be puréed, this makes a super family meal.

MAKES 15 PORTIONS

*1 chicken breast or 2 thighs, skinned
and off the bone
½ celery stalk, chopped
1 tomato, chopped
1 carrot, peeled and diced*

*2.5 cm/1 inch white leek, shredded
1 potato, peeled and diced
a sprig of parsley
250 ml/8 fl oz chicken stock
(see page 62)*

Cut the chicken into pieces and put it into a small flameproof casserole dish or saucepan together with the vegetables, parsley and chicken stock. Simmer gently for 30 minutes, then purée to the desired consistency.

☺ ☹

Chicken with Grapes and Courgettes

The addition of grapes to this recipe gives the chicken a little
sweetness which babies love. It is very simple to make and is
usually gobbled up pretty quickly.

MAKES 8 PORTIONS

*1 chicken breast or 2 thighs, skinned
and off the bone
150 ml/5 fl oz home-made chicken
stock (see page 62)*

*8 white grapes, peeled and pips
removed
1 courgette, washed and sliced
1 tablespoon baby rice*

Cut the chicken into pieces. Put all the ingredients except the baby
rice into a small saucepan and simmer for 30 minutes. Purée to
the desired consistency and thicken by stirring in the baby rice.

Chicken with Tomatoes

The tomatoes keep the chicken moist in this quick-to-prepare recipe.

MAKES 15 PORTIONS

*1 chicken breast or 2 thighs, skinned
and off the bone
1 carrot, peeled and chopped*

*1 small potato, peeled and chopped
400 g/14 oz can tomatoes, half the
juice drained off*

Cut the chicken into pieces. Put into a saucepan with the remaining ingredients and cook over a gentle heat for 15–20 minutes or until the chicken is cooked through and the vegetables soft. Put the mixture through a mouli for smaller babies or chop it up very finely for babies of nine months (and older).

Chicken Liver Special

Liver is one of the best foods you can give your baby. Find a liver recipe that your baby enjoys and make it again and again.

MAKES 6 PORTIONS

*2 chicken livers, cleaned and trimmed
1 dessertspoon chopped carrot
1 dessertspoon chopped white of leek
1 tablespoon chopped mushrooms*

*120 ml/4 fl oz chicken stock (see
page 62)
1 potato, peeled*

Cook the chicken livers together with the chopped vegetables in the stock for about 8 minutes over a low heat. Meanwhile, boil the potato until tender. Mash the potato. Purée the liver and vegetables together with the potato. The chicken stock makes this into quite a creamy purée.

PASTA

Tomato and Mushroom Pasta Sauce

You can buy very small shapes of pasta which your baby will not
need to chew. Allow 25 g/1 oz dry pasta for 3 portions and cook
according to packet instructions or longer for young babies.

MAKES 3 PORTIONS OF SAUCE

1 large tomato, skinned, seeded and
chopped
2 large basil leaves
15 g/¹/₂ oz margarine

4 button mushrooms, sliced
1 tablespoon milk
20 g/³/₄ oz Mozzarella cheese, cut
into small cubes

Fry the tomato with the basil leaves in margarine for about 2
minutes. Add the mushrooms and fry for a further 2 minutes. Add
the milk and the Mozzarella cubes. Stir well to melt the cheese, then
mix with cooked pasta and serve immediately. Purée the pasta and
sauce for young babies.

Green Pasta Sauce

MAKES 5 PORTIONS OF SAUCE

175 g/6 oz courgette
50 g/2 oz green beans

2 tablespoons chicken stock (see
page 62)

Wash and slice the courgettes and green beans. Steam them for 8–
10 minutes. Purée together with the chicken stock. Pour over
cooked pasta and serve.

Mushroom Pasta Sauce

Mushrooms go well with pasta and make a change from tomatoes.

MAKES 4 PORTIONS OF SAUCE

1 shallot, peeled and finely chopped
25 g/1 oz white of leek, shredded
a little margarine

150 g/5 oz button mushrooms,
washed and sliced
50 ml/2 fl oz chicken stock (see
page 62)

Sauté shallot and leek in margarine until golden. Add mushrooms and sauté for about 3 minutes. Pour in stock and simmer for about 5 minutes. Purée and pour over cooked pasta.

Tomato and Cheese Pasta Sauce

Butterfly-shaped pasta is fun for babies to grasp in their hands. You could add cooked broccoli florets or peas.

MAKES 4 PORTIONS OF SAUCE

15 g/¹/₂ oz margarine
1 large tomato, skinned, seeded and
chopped

20 g/³/₄ oz Cheddar cheese, grated
1 tablespoon cottage cheese
1 dessertspoon baby rice

Melt the margarine in a saucepan, add the tomato and cook over a low heat for 2 minutes. Remove the saucepan from the heat, stir in the cheeses and allow to melt into a sauce. Finally stir in the baby rice. Pour the sauce over cooked pasta and serve.

Napolitana Pasta Sauce

Try this good tomato sauce with some fresh ravioli – my children love ravioli stuffed with Ricotta and spinach.

MAKES 6 PORTIONS OF SAUCE

½ small onion, peeled and chopped
¼ garlic clove, peeled and chopped
25 g/1 oz white of leek, chopped
15 g/½ oz celery, chopped
½ small red or green sweet pepper, seeded and finely chopped

1 dessertspoon finely chopped parsley
15 g/½ oz margarine
6 medium tomatoes, skinned, seeded and chopped
1 dessertspoon chopped basil
2 tablespoons baby rice

Sauté the onion, garlic, leek, celery, pepper and parsley in the margarine until soft. Add the chopped tomato and basil to the saucepan and continue to cook for 2 minutes. Purée all the vegetables in a mouli or blender and stir in the baby rice to thicken the sauce. Pour over cooked pasta.

Popeye Pasta

MAKES 8 PORTIONS

100 g/4 oz spinach, trimmed
50 g/2 oz shell-shaped pasta

40 g/1½ oz Gruyère cheese, grated
2 tablespoons milk

Boil the spinach in a little water for about 5 minutes until tender. Meanwhile cook the pasta according to the instructions on the packet. Once the spinach is cooked press out all the excess water. Combine with the cheese, pasta and milk and blend to make into a purée or chop for older babies.

SIX TO NINE MONTH MEAL PLANNER

	Breakfast	Sleep	Lunch	Sleep	Tea	Bedtime
Day 1	Weetabix with milk Mashed banana	Milk	My First Chicken Purée Grated apple Juice	Milk	Leek and Potato Purée Pear Water or juice	Milk
Day 2	Ready Brek or porridge with milk and honey Fruit purée Milk	Milk	Plaice with Tomatoes and Potato Banana Juice	Milk	Pasta with Green Pasta Sauce Yoghurt Water or juice	Milk
Day 3	Apple and Baby Cereal Toast Milk	Milk	Cauliflower Cheese Grated pear Juice	Milk	Spinach and Potato Purée Rusk Water or juice	Milk
Day 4	Baby cereal with milk Dried Apricot Purée *Fromage frais*	Milk	Lentil Purée Peaches and Rice Juice	Milk	Minestrone Toast Water or juice	Milk
Day 5	Weetabix with milk Peaches, Apples and Pears	Milk	Pasta and Mushroom Sauce Baked Banana Milk	Milk	My First Chicken Purée Pear Water or juice	Milk
Day 6	Baby cereal with milk Cottage Cheese and Sharon Fruit	Milk	Courgette Gratin Home-made Fruit Jelly Milk	Milk	Chicken with Rice and Beans Apple Water	Milk
Day 7	Ready Brek with milk Cottage Cheese and Sharon Fruit	Milk	Chicken Liver Special Apple, Prune Custard Juice	Milk	Tasty Lettuce and Courgette Purée Papaya Water or juice	Milk

CHAPTER FOUR

NINE TO TWELVE MONTHS

Towards the end of the first year, babies' weight gain usually slows down quite dramatically. Quite often, babies who have been good eaters in the past become much more difficult to feed. Many refuse to be spoon-fed and want to assert their new-found independence, using their hands to feed themselves. My daughter at the age of ten months went through a phase of refusing to eat anything offered to her on a spoon. I was determined that she should eat the home-made purées I had prepared, so I gave her various finger foods like steamed carrots or strips of toast which I dipped into the purées. That way I succeeded in getting her to eat and enjoy them and everyone was happy.

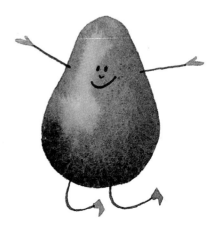

Mealtime Patience

Let your baby experiment by allowing him or her to use a spoon. Most of the food will probably end up on you or on the floor, but with practice your baby's aim will get better! Put a waterproof tablecloth under the high chair to catch the food that falls on the floor. It is probably best to have two bowls of food and two spoons, one which you use to spoon-feed your baby, the other (preferably a bowl which sticks to the table by suction) for your baby to play with. You will need lots of patience at meal times, as many babies are very easily distracted at this stage and prefer to play with their food rather than eat it. If all else fails I find that if you can attract their attention by giving them a small toy to hold, you can sometimes slip food into their mouths on a spoon and they will eat without really noticing what they are doing and forget to put up any resistance!

No child under the age of one needs to drink cow's milk. For drinks continue using formula or breast milk, which has a much lower salt content and is complete with essential vitamins. However, as solid food intake increases, milk need no longer form such a staple part of your child's diet, although they should still be drinking a minimum of 600 ml/1 pint of milk a day (or the equivalent as dairy products or in cooking). It is an important source of protein and calcium. Many mothers assume that when their baby cries it is because she wants more milk but often babies of this age are given *too much* milk and not enough solid food. If you fill your baby's stomach with milk when she really wants some solid food, you will not get a very satisfied baby.

If you have a juice extractor, you can make all sorts of wonderful fruit and vegetable drinks for your baby – try combinations like apple and banana juice. Your baby should now be drinking happily from a cup, the bottle kept for her bedtime drink of warm milk.

Your baby will be teething at this age and very often sore gums can put her off eating for a while. Don't worry, she will make up for this later that day or the next day. (Rubbing a teething gel on your baby's gums, or giving her something very cold to chew, can help relieve soreness and restore appetite.)

It is a good idea to eat something with your baby at meal times. There are some mothers who sit opposite their babies and try to spoon food into their mouths whilst eating nothing themselves. Babies are great mimics and more likely to enjoy eating if they see you tucking in as well.

The Foods to Choose

You can be a little more adventurous with the food that you make for your baby. It is a good idea now to develop her tastes for garlic and herbs, both of which are very healthy. Children tend to be less fussy eaters if they are introduced to a wide range of foods early. Again, if your baby dislikes certain foods, never force her to eat them; just leave out those foods and perhaps re-introduce them in a couple of months' time. Try also to vary the foods as much as possible, as this will lead to a more balanced diet. If you give your child a favourite food too often, it is possible she will go off it altogether.

Your baby can now eat berry fruits (but these should still be put through a mouli in the earlier stages to get rid of the indigestible seeds). Fruit jellies will be interesting for your baby to look at, feel and eat. Your baby will like fruit and vegetables that have been grated.

Oily fish can now be introduced; it contains iron and fat-soluble vitamins which white fish does not. All fish must obviously be very fresh. Chicken dishes can become more interesting in both texture and tastes and the types of pasta cooked can be large enough for the independent baby to pick up (butterflies, spirals, shells and animal shapes are good). Increase the quantity per serving of pasta to about 40 g/1½ oz, cooked (15–20 g/½–¾ oz dry).

Whenever possible, try to make the food look attractive on the plate. Choose contrasting colours and arrange the food in pretty shapes. You can use your imagination to make little faces or animals. Never pile too much food on to the plate but give a second helping – your baby will let you know in no uncertain terms if she wants more.

MEAT

A good red meat to introduce is liver, which is one of the most nutritious foods you can give your baby. It is the richest natural source of iron and is easily digested. If you do not like liver, try not to show it. Your reaction can easily put her off eating it. Be careful not to overcook liver or it will become tough and impossible for the baby to chew. Both my children enjoy eating liver, which surprised my husband and I (neither of us can bear the taste)!

Beef is the best red meat, I think, as it is less fatty than lamb. Although lamb and pork are both suitable around 1 year. Always choose lean cuts and make sure it is thoroughly cooked. After cooking minced meat for young babies, I find that if I chop it in a food processor for 30 seconds, it becomes much softer and easier to chew.

Textures and Quantities

It is easy to get into the habit of only giving your baby soft foods but you should try to vary the consistency of food that you give your baby. There is no need to purée all foods. Babies do not need teeth to be able to chew; gums do a great job on foods that are not too hard. Give some food mashed (fish), some grated (cheese), some diced (carrots) and some whole (pieces of chicken, slices of toast and pieces of raw fruit).

As far as quantities are concerned, you must let your baby's appetite be your guide. The portions in the recipes are a guide to what an average baby of this age would eat (two to three ice-cube-sized blocks, no longer singles).

You could start to freeze food in larger containers, like empty yoghurt pots, well covered with foil or polythene bags.

Finger Foods

By the age of nine months, your baby will probably want to start feeding herself. It is a good idea therefore to start giving her some foods that are easy for her to eat with her fingers. Finger foods are great for keeping your child occupied while you prepare her proper meal – or you could make a whole meal of finger foods.

Never leave your child unattended whilst eating. It is very easy for a baby to choke on even very small pieces of food. Avoid giving your baby whole nuts, fruits with stones, whole grapes, ice cubes, olives and any other foods that might get stuck in her throat.

RAW FRUIT

Always peel fruit and make sure any pips or stones have been removed. If your baby finds it difficult to chew, give soft fruits that melt in the mouth like bananas or peaches or grated fruits.

Berry and citrus fruits should only be given in very small quantities to start with. Remove as much of the pith as possible.

Many babies who are teething really enjoy biting into fruit. A banana put into the freezer for a few hours makes an excellent teething aid for young babies. Once your baby is able to hold food successfully give her larger pieces of fruit and encourage her to bite little bits off. (But don't let her *store* these in her mouth; on occasion I had to resort to opening my son's mouth and removing food which he refused to swallow!) If your baby has only a few teeth, then it is a good idea to give her grated fruit.

FRUITY IDEAS

apples, apricots, avocado pear, banana, cherries, clementines, blueberries, grapes, kiwi fruit, mango, melon, nectarine, orange, papaya, peach, pear, plum, raspberries, strawberries, tomato

---

DRIED FRUITS

Dried fruits are an excellent source of iron. If the fruit is too hard for your baby to chew, soften it first by soaking it in boiling water.

Do not give a lot of dried fruit as it can be difficult to digest, and laxative in effect. This is particularly true of raisins and sultanas (although babies love them!).

MORE FRUITY IDEAS
apple rings, banana chips, apricots, dates, peaches, pears, prunes, raisins, sultanas, yoghurt- or carob-coated raisins

---

VEGETABLES
To begin with, give your baby soft cooked vegetables cut into pieces that are easy for her to hold, and encourage her to bite off little pieces. (It is best to steam vegetables as this will help to preserve Vitamin C.) Gradually cook the vegetables for less time so that your baby gets used to having to chew harder. Once your baby has good coordination, she will enjoy picking up little vegetables like peas and sweetcorn.

Once your baby has mastered the art of feeding herself cooked vegetables, you can introduce carefully washed grated raw vegetables and sticks of raw vegetables. Even if your baby is unable to bite into these sticks, she will enjoy chewing on them as an aid to teething. In fact sticks of raw vegetables such as carrots and cucumber are very soothing for sore gums if they are chilled in the freezer or in iced water for a few minutes. Large pieces of raw vegetables are safer than small pieces as a baby will nibble off what she can manage, whereas a small piece put into

her mouth whole could cause her to choke if she tried to swallow it.

Try giving your baby corn on the cob once he or she can chew well. Cut the corn in half or into three pieces or look out for little mini-sized corn cobs in some supermarkets – just right for babies. Corn It is fun to eat and babies love to hold and chew it.

Vegetables are also very good dipped into sauces and purées. Try using some of the recipes for vegetable purées as dipping sauces.

VEGETABLE VARIETY
aubergine, beans (green), broccoli, Brussels sprouts, cabbage, carrots, cauliflower, celery, corn on the cob (and baby corn), courgettes, mangetout, mushrooms, peas, potato, swede, sweetcorn, sweet pepper, sweet potato

---

BREADS AND RUSKS
Pieces of toast, rusks and firm bread can be dipped into purées and sauces. Often a baby who refuses to be spoon-fed will eat her meal by sucking it off a rusk or a piece of toast.

Many baby rusks on the market contain as much sugar as a sweet biscuit and even so-called low-sugar rusks can contain more than 15 per cent sugar. It is very easy to make your own sugar-free alternative from wholemeal bread.

For home-made savoury rusks, simply cut a thick (1 cm/½ inch) slice of wholemeal (granary or rye) bread into three strips. Melt ⅛ teaspoon Marmite in 1 teaspoon boiling water, and brush this evenly over the bread strips. Bake in the oven preheated to 350°F(180°C)Gas 4 for 15 minutes. You can leave out the Marmite if your baby prefers and you can prepare a store of rusks in advance and keep them in an airtight container for 3 or 4 days.

Rice cakes come in all different flavours and are excellent for teething, as they seem to hold together well.

MINIATURE SANDWICHES

Little sandwiches cut into fingers, squares, small triangles or even animal shapes with a biscuit cutter are very popular with babies. There are some suggestions for fillings below and see the toddler section for a more exhaustive list (pages 186–187).

FILLING SUGGESTIONS
mashed banana
peanut butter and apple purée
chopped chicken with fruit chutney
cottage cheese and grated apple
cream cheese and strawberry jam
Marmite and grated cheese
cheese, tomato and grated cucumber
mashed sardines with tomato ketchup

BREAKFAST CEREALS

Babies love to pick up and eat little pieces of breakfast cereal. Try to choose cereals that are fortified with iron and vitamins and which do not have added sugar.

GOOD MORNING MUNCHIES
Cheerios, Cornflakes, Granola,
Shreddies

CHEESE

Start by giving your baby grated cheese or cut wafer-thin slices. Once she has mastered chewing, you can move on to chunks and strips of cheese. I have found that the following cheeses are especially popular: Cheddar, Mozzarella, Edam, Gouda, Emmenthal and Gruyère. Cream cheese and cottage cheeses are also very popular. Keep away from strong cheeses like blue cheese, Brie and Camembert. Always make sure that the cheese you give your baby is pasteurised.

PASTA

Pasta comes in all shapes and sizes, it is soft to chew and is very appealing to babies. I have given some recipes for pasta sauces but most of the vegetable purées can also be served with pasta. You can try sprinkling a little grated cheese over the pasta as well.

My children enjoy eating spaghetti as finger food!

MEAT

Slices or chunks of cooked chicken (or turkey) make great finger food. As well as plain pieces of chicken, try giving your baby chicken cooked in a sauce. Very often the sauce makes the chicken more tender and so it is easier for your baby to chew.

Miniature chicken balls are another favourite (try my recipe for Chicken and Apple Balls, page 98). Your baby may also enjoy chewing on miniature drumsticks. Remove the skin and make sure that your baby avoids eating any pieces of bone. There is a fine needle-like bone in all drumsticks which is potentially very dangerous – extra care needs to be taken with drumsticks.

Strips of sautéed liver make good finger food as they are easy to hold and soft to eat. Try, too, some miniature meatballs (see page 154). Pieces of steak and chunks of meat are generally too tough for young babies to chew.

FISH

Pieces of flaked white fish are good as they are low in fat, high in protein and easy for your child to chew. You can give them to your baby either plain or mixed with a sauce. Do take extra care when serving fish to your baby in any recipe to check the fish thoroughly for bones before you cook it and when flaking it.

Make your own fish fingers and fish balls (see pages 94, 133–134).

Breakfast

The first meal of the day is important to all of us after a night's fasting, particularly so to energetic babies and toddlers!

Recipes can now contain more interesting and more nutritious grains. Wheatgerm is particularly good and can be sprinkled on to cereals or yoghurt. Mixing cereals and fruit makes a delicious and nutritious start to the day. Many of the home-made cereals can be mixed with apple juice instead of milk.

Recent research has shown that oat bran (available in health-food stores) can prevent the build up of cholesterol in the blood (even in young children) and you can easily include this in your baking for the whole family.

Highly refined, sugar-coated cereals should be avoided. Do not be fooled by the list of added vitamins on the side of the packet – unprocessed cereals are much healthier for your child.

Individual packets of cereals are great fun for your baby. She can nibble from the box and once it is empty it is fun to play with too. Choosing different cereals to combine can brighten the morning.

There are also some recipes in the toddler baking and fruit dessert sections which make excellent breakfast food: Bran Muffins with Apples and Raisins (page 175); Funny Shape Biscuits (page 178), Snow-Covered Fruit Salad (page 165), or Banana Split (page 164).

BREAKFAST

Fruity Swiss Muesli

You can vary the fruit in this muesli, adding, for example, sliced peaches or bananas instead of grapes. It can be served with or without milk. Make this for the whole family.

MAKES 6 ADULT PORTIONS

75 g/3 oz wheatgerm
75 g/3 oz rolled oats
475 ml/16 fl oz unsweetened apple juice
2 teaspoons lemon juice

1 tablespoon honey
2 apples, peeled, cored and chopped
2 pears, peeled, cored and chopped
500 g/18 oz grapes, halved and seeded

Combine the wheatgerm, rolled oats and apple juice, cover and refrigerate overnight. Next morning, stir in the lemon juice, honey, chopped apples and pears, place in a food processor and switch on for 30 seconds. Put the muesli into a serving bowl and add the grapes.

Fruity Yoghurt

Many commercial fruit yoghurts have a lot of added sugar. It is easy to make your own, adding a combination of your baby's favourite foods.

MAKES 2 ADULT PORTIONS

2 tablespoons mixed ripe chopped fruit
¹/₂ teaspoon vanilla essence
1 teaspoon honey

150 g/5 oz natural yoghurt
2 tablespoons apple juice
1 teaspoon wheatgerm

Mix everything together except for the wheatgerm which you sprinkle on top. (Purée the fruit first for younger babies.)

Easy Fruit Brunch

This takes a minute to prepare and is quite delicious.

MAKES 4 ADULT PORTIONS

2 bananas, peeled
225 g/8 oz natural yoghurt
2 tablespoons cream cheese
2 tablespoons double cream

2 teaspoons honey (optional)
25 g/1 oz tinned prunes, stoned
a pinch powdered cinnamon

Simply mix all the ingredients together except for the cinnamon and a few reserved banana slices and blend until smooth. Decorate with slices of banana and the cinnamon.

Fruit Compote

I like to serve this cold with yoghurt for breakfast but it could also be served hot with ice-cream for dessert.

MAKES 4 ADULT PORTIONS

125 g/4½ oz each of stoned prunes and dried apricots
65 g/2½ oz each of dried apples, dried figs and sultanas
175 ml/6 fl oz orange juice

200 ml/7 fl oz water
¼ cinnamon stick
1½ fresh pears, peeled, cored and diced
75 g/3 oz natural yoghurt

Combine dried fruits and all the other ingredients except for the fresh pears and yoghurt. Put dried fruits, liquid and spice into a heavy-bottomed saucepan, bring to the boil, reduce heat and simmer, covered, for 30 minutes. Add the diced fresh pears and simmer for another 10 minutes. Discard the cinnamon stick and leave compote to cool.

Serve cold with the yoghurt.

Cornflakes with Apples

MAKES 2 PORTIONS

2 tablespoons cornflakes
2 tablespoons apple purée (see page 24)

2 tablespoons natural yoghurt
1 teaspoon honey (optional)

Put all the ingredients into a food processor and blend until well mixed (about 30 seconds).

Apple Muesli

You can vary the recipe by combining different fruits and, later on, your toddler may enjoy a few well-chopped nuts.

MAKES 4–5 ADULT PORTIONS

100 g/4 oz porridge oats
2 tablespoons sultanas
300 ml/10 fl oz freshly squeezed
orange juice

2 eating apples, peeled, cored and
grated
milk to mix
1 tablespoon honey

Mix the oats, sultanas and orange juice in a bowl, cover and leave to soak overnight in the fridge. In the morning, stir in the grated apple and enough milk and honey to make the muesli soft and moist.

☺ ☹

Mixed Cereal Muesli

As your child gets older you can let her help make up her very own muesli recipe using her favourite breakfast cereals and fruit.

MAKES 2 ADULT PORTIONS

1 tablespoon Cheerios
1 tablespoon Bran Flakes
1 Weetabix, crushed
4 slices of canned peaches, cut into
chunks

½ tablespoon raisins
½ small apple, peeled, cored and cut
into chunks
1 dessertspoon wheatgerm

Mix all the ingredients together, varying the combination of cereals and fruits to your taste and serve with milk.

Cornflakes with Yoghurt

I find that children love their own individual portions of food, and my two like to eat dry cornflakes from the miniature packets. If I put cornflakes into a bowl and add milk, they won't touch them! This and Cornflakes with Apples (page 81) are good for older babies who are lazy at chewing and prefer their food puréed.

MAKES 2 PORTIONS

2 tablespoons cornflakes   *2 teaspoons strawberry jam, warmed*
150 g/5 oz natural or vanilla yoghurt

Put all the ingredients into a food processor and blend until well mixed (about 30 seconds).

Matzo Brei

For those of you who have never heard of *matzo*, it is a large square of unleavened bread similar to crispbread. When uncooked, it is very brittle and Nicholas loves to snap it into pieces and strew it all over the floor. This is why I prefer to give it to him cooked!

MAKES 2 ADULT PORTIONS

1 matzo   *25 g/1 oz margarine*
1 egg, beaten   *a pinch of sugar (optional)*

Break the *matzo* into small pieces and soak for a couple of minutes in cold water. Squeeze out the excess water then add the *matzo* to the beaten egg. Melt the margarine in a frying pan until sizzling and fry the *matzo* on both sides. Sprinkle with sugar if wished.

French Toast

French toast can be served with a variety of toppings such as maple syrup, honey, peanut butter or jam. For a change, you could add cinnamon instead of vanilla, then blend a ripe banana with the milk and soak the bread in the banana mixture before frying.

MAKES 2 ADULT PORTIONS

1 egg
120 ml/4 fl oz milk
1/4 teaspoon vanilla essence

2 slices white, raisin or wholemeal bread
a little margarine

Beat the egg lightly and add milk and vanilla. Soak the bread in the mixture. Melt the margarine in a frying pan and fry the slices of bread on both sides until golden brown. Wholemeal bread slices are more fragile than white bread and can break very easily.

Cheese Scramble

You could use cottage cheese instead of Cheddar cheese.

MAKES 1 ADULT PORTION

1 egg
1 tablespoon milk
15 g/1/2 oz margarine

1 tablespoon Cheddar cheese, finely grated
1 tomato, skinned and seeded

Beat the egg with the milk. Melt the margarine over a low heat then add the egg mixture. Cook slowly, stirring all the time. When the mixture has thickened and looks soft and creamily set, add the cheese and chopped tomato. Serve immediately.

FRUIT

Baked Apples with Raisins

Cooking apples have a better flavour but eating apples are sweeter.
You can use either for this recipe. The apples are delicious served
with ice cream or custard.

MAKES 6 PORTIONS

2 apples
120 ml/4 fl oz apple juice or water
2 tablespoons raisins

a little powdered cinnamon
1 dessertspoon honey or maple syrup
(if using cooking apples)
a little butter or margarine

Core the apples and prick the skins with a fork to stop them
bursting. Put the apples in an ovenproof dish and pour the apple
juice or water around the base. Put 1 tablespoon of the raisins into the
centre of each apple, sprinkle with cinnamon and pour over honey or
maple syrup (if using cooking apples). Top each with a little butter.
Bake in an oven preheated to 350°F(180°C)Gas 4 for about 45
minutes.

For young babies scoop out the
pulp of the apple and purée
roughly with the raisins and some
of the juices from the dish.

Apple and Blackberry

Blackberries and apples make a delicious combination, and the blackberries (which are rich in Vitamin C) turn the apples dark red. This also makes a super filling for a crumble (see page 167).

MAKES 8 PORTIONS

2 cooking apples, peeled, cored and sliced

100 g/4 oz blackberries
caster sugar to taste

Cook the apples with the blackberries in a saucepan with the sugar and 1 tablespoon water. Cook until the apples are soft (about 10 minutes). Put the fruit through a mouli to make into a smooth purée.

Rice Pudding with Peaches

MAKES 8–10 PORTIONS

600 ml/1 pint milk
60 g/2¼ oz pudding rice
15 g/½ oz each of vanilla and brown sugars, or 25 g/1 oz caster sugar

1 cinnamon stick
2 ripe peaches, skinned
1 heaped tablespoon raisins
120 ml/4 fl oz peach or apple juice

Bring the milk to the boil, add the rice, sugar and cinnamon stick and simmer, stirring occasionally, for about 1 hour, 40 minutes until the rice is tender. Alternatively, bake in a buttered dish for about 2 hours at 300°F(150°C)Gas 2, stirring after 30 minutes.

Meanwhile purée the peaches, and simmer the raisins in the peach or apple juice. When the rice pudding is cooked, stir in the peach purée, raisins and fruit juice.

Fresh Pear with Semolina

This recipe is also good with apricots or apple purée with cinnamon. If you do not have any semolina, you can add a finely crushed rusk to the milk (which does not need to be boiled).

MAKES 2 PORTIONS

1 tablespoon semolina
120 ml/4 fl oz milk

1 ripe pear, peeled, cored and sliced
1 teaspoon clear honey (optional)

Put the semolina and milk in a saucepan, bring to the boil and simmer for 3–4 minutes. Add the pear and honey, if using, then put all the ingredients through a mouli to make a purée or chop the pear finely.

Strawberry Rice Pudding

The secret of a good rice pudding is long, slow, gentle cooking. Make it after breakfast and it will be ready in time for lunch.

MAKES 6 PORTIONS

50 g/2 oz short-grain brown rice
1/4 teaspoon vanilla essence
1 dessertspoon strawberry jam

600 ml/1 pint milk
a little butter

Put the rice, vanilla and strawberry jam into a buttered ovenproof dish. Pour over the milk, dot with the butter, and cook in an oven heated to 300°F(150°C)Gas 2 for 3 hours. Stir the mixture well after 30 minutes. Serve with extra strawberry jam whirled into the rice pudding.

Cheese and Raisin Delight

This makes a delicious combination and is very nutritious.

MAKES 2 PORTIONS

25 g/1 oz Gruyère cheese
½ small apple, peeled

15 g/½ oz raisins
1 tablespoon fromage frais

Grate the Gruyère cheese and apple and mix in the raisins and fromage frais. For young babies who do not chew, put all the ingredients in a blender for about 1 minute.

Yoghurt with Dried Fruit

Serve this warm with some vanilla ice cream as a special treat.

MAKES 12 PORTIONS

50 g/2 oz dried apples
175 ml/6 fl oz natural apple juice
1 ripe pear, peeled, cored and chopped

50 g/2 oz canned prunes, stoned and drained
150 g/5 oz natural yoghurt

Put the apples in a saucepan with the apple juice, bring to the boil and simmer for about 20 minutes. After 10 minutes add the pear pieces. Drain the apples and pear and put through a mouli together with the prunes. Add the yoghurt and mix it together with the fruit in a blender.

VEGETABLES

Oscar's Delight

So called because this recipe is the same green colour as 'Oscar', the character from *Sesame Street*. If my son believes this is Oscar's favourite food he is much more likely to eat it himself. Calling food funny names is another way to encourage children to eat.

MAKES 10 PORTIONS

175 g/6 oz courgettes, trimmed,
washed and sliced
100 g/4 oz cauliflower florets

75 g/3 oz broccoli, cut into florets
25 g/1 oz Cheddar cheese, grated
1 egg yolk

Steam the vegetables for 7 minutes until tender, then purée with the cheese and egg yolk. Bake in a greased dish at 350°F(180°C)Gas 4 for 15–20 minutes.

Gratin of Carrots

You can also try this recipe with celery or fennel.

MAKES 6 PORTIONS

100 g/4 oz carrots
1 egg
120 ml/4 fl oz milk

40 g/1½ oz Gruyère cheese, grated
½ teaspoon fresh tarragon (optional)
a little margarine

Make a carrot purée (see page 25), add remaining ingredients and bake as in recipe above for 10–15 minutes.

Lentil and Vegetable Purée

This makes a delicious purée which my nine-month-old daughter loved. Lentils are an excellent source of protein and very easy to cook.

MAKES 10 PORTIONS

1 medium onion, finely chopped
75 g/3 oz celery, trimmed and chopped
100 g/4 oz carrots, peeled and chopped

oil or margarine for frying
50 g/2 oz split red lentils
600 ml/1 pint vegetable stock (see page 33) or water

Fry the onion, celery and carrot in a little oil for about 10 minutes until tender. Add the lentils and pour over the stock or water. Simmer covered, for 20 minutes. Make into a purée in a blender or put through a mouli. ☺ ☹

Multi-Coloured Casserole

Babies love the bright colours and miniature size of these vegetables. It makes eating fun, and is a good lesson in finger control.

MAKES 6 PORTIONS

25 ml/1 fl oz olive oil
4 shallots, peeled and finely chopped
1 red sweet pepper, seeded and finely chopped

150 g/5 oz frozen peas
275 g/10 oz frozen sweetcorn
100 g/4 oz Cheddar cheese, grated
1 tablespoon finely chopped parsley

Heat the oil in a frying pan, add the shallots and red pepper and cook for 3 minutes. Meanwhile cook the peas and sweetcorn in boiling water for about 4 minutes, then drain. Put the vegetables into an ovenproof dish, sprinkle with the cheese and parsley and bake in the oven preheated to 350°F(180°C)Gas 4 for 15 minutes.

Cabbage Surprise

This is a delicious recipe and very simple to prepare. It makes a great lunchtime meal for the whole family; just increase the quantities, sprinkle with extra grated cheese, either Cheddar or Parmesan and brown under the grill before serving. Alternatively, mix all the ingredients together and bake in the oven at 350°F(180°C)Gas 4 for 15 minutes.

MAKES 6 PORTIONS

25 g/1 oz brown rice
75 g/3 oz cabbage, shredded
*1 tomato, skinned, seeded and
    chopped*

a little margarine or oil
50 g/2 oz Cheddar cheese, grated

Cook the rice in water until quite soft (about 25 minutes). Boil the cabbage in water for about 5 minutes or until tender. Sauté the tomato in a little margarine, add the well drained cabbage and continue to cook for a further 2 minutes. Stir in the grated cheese and cook over a low heat until all the cheese has melted. Mix the cabbage, tomato and cheese together with the cooked rice and chop it into small pieces.

Vegetables in Cheese Sauce

MAKES 12 PORTIONS

100 g/4 oz cauliflower florets
1 carrot, peeled and thinly sliced
50 g/2 oz podded peas
100 g/4 oz courgettes, washed and sliced

Cheese sauce
25 g/1 oz margarine
1½ tablespoons plain flour
120 ml/4 fl oz milk
40 g/1½ oz Cheddar cheese, grated

Steam the cauliflower and carrot for 6 minutes, then add the peas and courgettes and cook for a further 4 minutes. For a young baby cook the vegetables until they are soft.

Meanwhile make the cheese sauce in the usual way (see page 59). Mash, chop or purée the vegetables with the sauce.

Green Fingers

French beans make great finger food and they are especially good with this tasty tomato sauce. To make them more appealing to your baby, arrange them in a pattern on the plate.

MAKES 5 PORTIONS

1 small onion, finely chopped
a little margarine
175 g/6 oz French beans, trimmed

2 medium tomatoes, skinned
½ tablespoon tomato paste
25 g/1 oz Gruyère cheese, grated

Sauté the onion in a little margarine for about 4 minutes until soft but not golden. Meanwhile steam the beans for 6–8 minutes until tender. Seed and chop tomatoes, mix them with the onions, tomato paste and cheese. Pour the sauce over the beans or chop coarsely.

FISH

Plaice with Herbs

Easy to make and all the flavour is sealed in a parcel.

MAKES 3 PORTIONS

1 fillet of plaice
1 teaspoon olive oil
1 medium tomato, skinned, seeded and chopped
1 small courgette, washed and sliced

1 dessertspoon chopped chives
1 sprig each of parsley, tarragon and chervil (optional)
a squeeze of lemon juice

Place the fish fillet on a piece of oiled aluminium foil. Mix all the remaining ingredients together and place on top of the fish. Wrap up securely. Cook in the oven preheated to 350°F(180°C)Gas 4 for about 12 minutes or until the fish just flakes with a fork. Remove the herb sprigs and mash with a fork.

Fingers of Sole

These fingers of sole are fun for babies and toddlers to eat, and make great finger food. They can be served plain or you can dip them into a home-made tomato sauce. Simply purée 3 skinned and seeded tomatoes with a sautéed shallot, 1 tablespoon tomato purée, 1 dessertspoon of milk and a teaspoon of finely chopped basil. These 'fish fingers' are much better for your child than commercial ones which are full of colouring and additives. If you are not using all the fingers at once, it is best to freeze them before they are cooked. You can then take out as many fingers as you need for a freshly cooked meal.

Crushed cornflakes also make a delicious coating for other types of fish like haddock or cod.

MAKES 8 PORTIONS

1 shallot, peeled and finely chopped
1 dessertspoon lemon juice
1 tablespoon vegetable oil
1 sole, filleted and skinned

1 egg
1 dessertspoon milk
plain flour
crushed cornflakes
a little butter or margarine for frying

Mix together the chopped shallot, lemon juice and oil. Marinate the fish fillets in this mixture for 1 hour. Remove the fillets from the marinade. Cut them into four or five diagonal strips, depending on the size of the sole. Beat the egg together with the milk. Dip the strips first into the flour, then the egg and milk and finally the crushed cornflakes. Fry the fingers in butter until golden brown on both sides. They should take no more than 5 minutes to cook.

Fillets of Sole with Grapes

Fruit and fish mix very well together and the sweetness of the grapes in this recipe gives the sole a delicious taste that babies love.

MAKES 4 PORTIONS

2 fillets of sole (a ½ sole)
1 small shallot, peeled and finely chopped
25 g/1 oz mushrooms, washed and finely sliced

1 teaspoon chopped parsley
150 ml/5 fl oz milk
15 g/½ oz margarine
1 dessertspoon plain flour
6 grapes, skinned, halved and seeded

Put the fillets of sole in a dish together with the shallot, mushrooms and parsley and pour over the milk. Cook in an oven preheated to 350°F(180°C)Gas 4 for 8–10 minutes or cover with a lid and microwave on High for 3½ minutes. Once the fish is cooked, drain off and reserve the milk.

Use the margarine, the flour and the flavoured milk to make a thick sauce in the usual way (see page 59). Chop the grapes into the sauce. Chop the fish into pieces and pour the sauce over the fish.

Haddock with Vegetables in a Cheese Sauce

Babies love bright colours and the yellow of the sweetcorn with the red and green of the tomato and leek makes this dish look attractive. Be careful not to overcook the fish or it will become dry. Once cooked, the fish will just flake with a fork and, mixed with the cheese sauce, will be nice and soft for your baby to eat.

MAKES 6 PORTIONS

175 g/6 oz fillet of haddock, skinned
a little margarine
a squeeze of lemon
25 g/1 oz leek, washed and shredded
50 g/2 oz frozen sweetcorn
1 tomato, skinned, seeded and chopped

Cheese sauce
15 g/½ oz margarine
1 dessertspoon plain flour
175 ml/6 fl oz milk
25 g/1 oz Cheddar cheese, grated

Put the fish into a dish, dot with margarine and add a squeeze of lemon juice. Cover with a lid and microwave for 4 minutes on High. Alternatively cook the fish in an oven preheated to 350°F(180°C)Gas 4 for 8–10 minutes.

Sauté the leek in a little margarine for 2 minutes. Cook the sweetcorn in boiling water until tender (about 6 minutes). Make the cheese sauce in the usual way (see page 59). Flake the fish with a fork and stir it, the vegetables and tomato into the cheese sauce.

Salmon with a Creamy Chive Sauce

Salmon is easy to cook. It can be cooked very quickly in the microwave but here I have wrapped it in aluminium foil with some vegetables and herbs and cooked it more slowly to bring out the flavour.

MAKES 5 PORTIONS

100 g/4 oz fillet of salmon
1 dessertspoon lemon juice
½ small onion, peeled and sliced
½ bay leaf
1 button mushroom, washed and sliced
½ small tomato, cut into chunks
a sprig of parsley
a little butter

Chive sauce
7 g/¼ oz margarine
1 dessertspoon plain flour
150 ml/5 fl oz milk
cooking liquid from the fish
1 dessertspoon snipped chives

Wrap the salmon in aluminium foil with the rest of the ingredients and bake in an oven preheated to 325°F(160°C)Gas 3 for 20 minutes. Meanwhile, make a thick white sauce, using the margarine, flour and milk in the usual way (see page 59).

Once the salmon is cooked, remove it from the foil, strain off the cooking liquid and add this to the white sauce. Finally, stir the chopped chives into the sauce. Flake the salmon and pour the chive sauce over it.

CHICKEN

Chicken with Apple

The sweetness of the apple makes this chicken recipe especially appealing to babies.

MAKES 2 PORTIONS

½ apple, peeled, cored and sliced
½ small cooked chicken breast, chopped

a little margarine
a squeeze of lemon juice

Cook the apple in a saucepan over a low heat with a little water until soft. Mix the chicken together with the mashed apple. Add the margarine and lemon juice.

Chicken and Apple Balls

This is a tasty recipe, very easy to make and the apple blends really well with the chicken to bring out the flavour and keep it moist. These little balls make great finger food.

MAKES 10 GOLF-BALLS

3 breasts of chicken or 6 thighs, off the bone and skinned
1 large eating apple, peeled
1 tablespoon lemon juice
½ small onion, peeled and finely chopped

1 tablespoon chopped fresh thyme or parsley
1 small egg, beaten
pinch mixed dried herbs
plain flour
vegetable oil

Chop the chicken very finely in the food processor and grate the apple. Mix the lemon juice with the apple. Combine chicken, apple, onion, fresh herbs and enough beaten egg to moisten. Mix well together and season with a pinch of mixed herbs. Form into little balls and roll in flour. Heat oil in a frying pan and when it is really hot, shallow-fry the balls until they are golden and cooked through (about 6 minutes).

☺ ☹

Bang Bang Chicken

So called because my son likes to help when I flatten the chicken by banging it with a mallet! You can prepare these chicken fingers in advance. Before frying the chicken, cut it into strips, wrap each strip separately and freeze. Just take one or two strips out of the freezer and fry them for freshly cooked chicken.

MAKES 8 PORTIONS

2 chicken breasts, skinned and off the bone
3 slices wholemeal bread
1 tablespoon grated Parmesan cheese (optional)

1 tablespoon chopped parsley (optional)
2 tablespoons plain flour
1 egg, beaten
vegetable oil

Cover the chicken with greaseproof paper and flatten with a mallet or rolling pin. Make breadcrumbs from the slices of bread in a food processor. If you are using the Parmesan and parsley, mix these together with the breadcrumbs in a bowl.

Dip the chicken into the flour, then into the egg and then finally into the breadcrumbs. Fry in oil for 3–4 minutes each side until golden on the outside and cooked through. Drain well. Cool. Cut the chicken breasts into strips and let your baby hold them as he eats.

Chicken in Tomato Sauce

This is good served with some rice.

MAKES 3 PORTIONS

*1 chicken breast, on the bone and
skinned
a little margarine
1 onion, peeled and finely chopped
2.5 cm/1 inch celery stalk, finely
chopped
1 tablespoon plain flour
1 dessertspoon tomato purée*

*85 ml/3 fl oz chicken stock (see page
62)
50 g/2 oz button mushrooms, washed
and sliced
1 large tomato, skinned and chopped
small
1 bouquet garni*

Fry the chicken until golden in a little margarine (about 5 minutes). Meanwhile fry the onion and celery until soft in a little margarine. Add the flour to the onion and celery and stir to make a paste. Stir in the tomato purée and chicken stock and bring to the boil. Fry the sliced mushrooms in a little margarine for 2 minutes.

Put the chicken into a small casserole dish, pour over the tomato sauce and add the chopped tomato, the mushrooms and bouquet garni. Cook in an oven preheated to 350°F(180°C)Gas 4 for 35 minutes. Remove the *bouquet garni*, take the chicken off the bone and cut into chunks or strips.

☺ ☹

Chicken with Summer Vegetables

In the summer, you can often find different varieties of squash – some are round, some green and some yellow. They are all delicious, but this recipe can also be made simply with courgettes.

MAKES 3 PORTIONS

1 chicken breast, on the bone and skinned
vegetable oil
120 ml/4 fl oz chicken stock (see page 62)
2 courgettes, washed and finely chopped

¼ red sweet pepper, seeded and finely chopped
1 shallot, peeled and finely chopped
a small piece of yellow squash, finely chopped
½ tablespoon chopped basil

Fry the chicken breast in a little oil for about 5 minutes. Pour the chicken stock over and simmer for 10 minutes. Add the finely chopped vegetables and basil, cover and simmer for a further 10 minutes.

Remove the chicken from the bone, cut flesh into very small pieces and serve it with the vegetables and chicken stock. If necessary you can make it into a rough purée in a blender or food processor.

Chicken with Cornflakes

Cornflakes are very versatile, and I often use them instead of breadcrumbs to coat both chicken and fish.

MAKES 6 PORTIONS

1 egg, beaten
2 tablespoons milk
50 g/2 oz cornflakes, crushed

2 chicken breasts, skinned and off the bone
25 g/1 oz margarine, melted

Mix together the beaten egg and milk in a shallow dish. In a separate dish, spread out the cornflake crumbs. Dip the chicken breasts first into the egg and then coat with the cornflakes. Put the chicken into a greased ovenproof dish and pour over the melted margarine. Bake for about 1 hour in the oven preheated to 350°F(180°C)Gas 4.

Chicken with Winter Vegetables

This is quick and easy to prepare and has a delicious rich chicken flavour. It is good with mashed potato.

MAKES 6 PORTIONS

2 chicken breasts, on the bone and skinned
a little flour
vegetable oil
1 small onion, peeled and finely chopped

1 white of leek, washed and sliced
1 carrot, peeled and sliced
1 celery stalk, trimmed and sliced
300 ml/10 fl oz chicken stock (see page 62)

Cut the chicken breasts in half, roll them in flour and brown them in a little oil for 3–4 minutes. In another frying pan, sauté the onion and leek in a little oil for 5 minutes until soft and golden. Put the chicken into a casserole together with all the vegetables and the stock. Cook in an oven preheated to 350°F(180°C)Gas 4 for 1 hour, stirring half-way through.

Take the chicken off the bone and chop it into little pieces with the vegetables or purée it together with the cooking liquid in a mouli or blender.

☺ ☹

RED MEATS

Beef Casserole with Carrots

The secret for a delicious rich taste is to cook the meat for a long time so that it is very tender and has a good flavour from the onions and carrots. Increase the Marmite for toddlers.

MAKES 10 PORTIONS

2 medium onions, peeled and sliced
vegetable oil
350 g/12 oz lean stewing beef,
trimmed and cut into small chunks
2 medium carrots, peeled and sliced

1 beef stock cube, crumbled or 1
teaspoon Marmite
1 tablespoon chopped parsley
600 ml/1 pint water
2 large potatoes, cut into quarters

Fry the onion till golden in a little oil, then add the meat chunks and brown. Transfer the meat and onions to a small casserole and add all the rest of the ingredients except for the potatoes. Cook, covered, in an oven preheated to 350°F(180°C)Gas 4 for 30 minutes, then turn down the heat and cook for a further 3½ hours at 325°F(160°C)Gas 3. One hour before you finish cooking the meat, add the potato.

Chop the meat quite finely in a food processor or blender so that it is easy for your baby to chew. If the meat gets too dry whilst cooking, add a little extra water. You can also add mushrooms and tomatoes to this recipe for variation and they should be added half an hour before the end of cooking time.

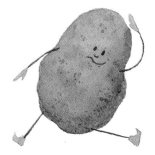

Liver Casserole

I have found that mothers who do not like liver themselves seldom cook it for their children. But liver is very good for children; it is easy to digest, a good source of iron and is also very easy to cook. I must admit that I dislike the taste of liver having been forced to eat it as a child at school but, to my great surprise, my one-year-old son adored it. This recipe is good served with mashed potato.

MAKES 8 PORTIONS

1 small onion, peeled and chopped
vegetable oil
1 large or 2 small carrots, peeled and chopped
225 g/8 oz calf's liver, trimmed and sliced

2 large tomatoes, skinned, seeded and chopped
1 tablespoon vegetable stock (see page 33)
1 dessertspoon chopped parsley

Fry the onion in a little oil until transparent. Add the chopped carrot and continue to fry for about 4 minutes. Add the liver, tomato, stock and parsley. Simmer over a low heat for 15–20 minutes. Cut the liver into small pieces or blend for a few seconds to make a rough purée.

Savoury Veal Casserole

A delicious casserole of veal, vegetables and fresh herbs – just increase the quantities for a meal the whole family can enjoy.

MAKES 3 PORTIONS

1 small onion, finely chopped
1 carrot, scraped and sliced
1/2 stick celery, sliced
vegetable oil

100 g/4 oz lean veal for stewing
1 sprig rosemary
1 sprig parsley
120 ml/4 fl oz water

Fry the onion, carrot and celery in a little oil for 3 minutes. Cut the veal into chunks and put it into a saucepan with the vegetables, herbs and the water. Simmer slowly, covered for 1 hour (stirring once). Remove the herbs and roughly chop the veal and vegetables in a food processor.

☺ ☹

Special Steak

This recipe makes a very good introduction to red meat for your baby. Later you could merely chop the steak (fillet or rump) in the food processor so that it is easy to chew and more palatable for your baby. You could also leave out the potato.

MAKES 3 PORTIONS

1 medium potato, peeled
a little margarine
1 shallot or onion, peeled and finely chopped
50 g/2 oz fillet steak

50 g/2 oz button mushrooms, washed and chopped
1 medium tomato, skinned, seeded and chopped
2 tablespoons milk

Boil the potato until soft. Melt the margarine and brush on to a piece of aluminium foil. Sprinkle over the chopped shallot and place under a hot grill for about 4 minutes or until the shallot has become soft. Brush the steak with the chopped shallot and margarine, and sprinkle with the chopped mushrooms and tomato. Cook under the grill for 3 minutes each side. Mash the potato together with the milk, then purée in a blender together with the steak. Put through a mouli if you want to make a very smooth purée.

☺ ☹

Mini Shepherd's Pie

Shepherd's pie was always a great 'comfort food' on a winter's evening when I was a child. Try this tasty recipe for your baby (and see page 155 for a more grown-up version).

MAKES 4 PORTIONS

1/4 onion, peeled and finely chopped
1 small piece of garlic, finely chopped (optional)
cooking oil
1/4 green sweet pepper, seeded and finely chopped
100 g/4 oz lean minced beef

1 teaspoon each of chopped parsley and basil
1 tomato, skinned, seeded and chopped
1 medium potato, peeled
2 tablespoons milk

Fry the onion and garlic in a little oil for about 5 minutes until soft. Add the green pepper and fry for a further 3 minutes. Add the meat, parsley and basil and cook the meat, stirring, until it turns brown. Add the tomato and 1 tablespoon water, cover and simmer for 15–20 minutes until the meat is very tender.

Meanwhile, cook the potato until tender and mash together with the milk. Put the potato and meat through a mouli to make a very smooth purée.

Tasty Rice with Meat and Vegetables

MAKES 8 PORTIONS

¹/₂ onion, peeled and finely chopped
1 carrot, scrubbed and finely chopped
vegetable oil
225 g/8 oz lean minced beef
1¹/₂ tablespoons tomato ketchup
a few drops of Worcestershire sauce

Rice
50 g/2 oz brown rice
450 ml/15 fl oz chicken stock (see
page 62)
¹/₂ red pepper, seeded and finely
chopped
75 g/3 oz peas, fresh or frozen

Put the rice into a saucepan and cover with the chicken stock. Bring to the boil and simmer for 15 minutes. Add the red pepper and peas and cook for a further 5 minutes.

Meanwhile sauté the onion and carrot in a little vegetable oil for 3 minutes. Add the minced meat and cook, stirring, until browned. Stir in the tomato ketchup and Worcestershire sauce and cook over a gentle heat for 10 minutes. Chop the meat in a food processor for about 30 seconds to make it easier for your baby to chew.

Put the meat into a saucepan, stir in the rice (with the chicken stock) and cook over a gentle heat for 3–4 minutes.

PASTA

Salmon and Vegetable Tagliatelle

Pasta combines with fish well – use tinned or fresh salmon.

MAKES 8 PORTIONS OF SAUCE

50 g/2 oz button mushrooms
1 large tomato, skinned, seeded and chopped
a little margarine or oil
1 small carrot
75 g/3 oz broccoli florets
50 g/2 oz mangetout, trimmed and cut into strips
75 g/3 oz sweetcorn
100 g/4 oz tinned salmon, drained

Cheese Sauce
15 g/½ butter
1 tablespoon flour
½ teaspoon dried mustard
250 ml/8 fl oz milk
50 g/2 oz mature Cheddar cheese, grated
½ tablespoon chopped parsley
1 tablespoon freshly grated Parmesan

Fry the mushrooms and tomato for 3 minutes in a little margarine or oil. Cut the carrot into small strips. Steam with the broccoli and mangetout until tender crisp. Add the sweetcorn and cook for the last 3 minutes. Make the cheese sauce in the usual way (see page 59). Add the vegetables and salmon, mix with cooked tagliatelle and sprinkle with Parmesan. Chop finely or coarsely.

Bolognese Sauce with Aubergine

Spaghetti (about 40 g/1½ oz cooked, 15–20 g/½–¾ oz dry per serving) is a firm favourite with older babies and toddlers.

MAKES 12 PORTIONS OF SAUCE

1 aubergine, peeled and sliced
salt
1 medium onion, finely chopped
¼ garlic clove, finely chopped
vegetable oil
450 g/1 lb lean minced meat
2 tablespoons tomato purée

4 tomatoes, skinned, seeded and
chopped
¼ teaspoon mixed herbs
2 tablespoons plain flour
450 ml/15 fl oz chicken stock (see
page 62)
100 g/4 oz mushrooms, sliced

Sprinkle the aubergine with a little salt and leave to drain for 30 minutes. Rinse well and pat dry. Sauté the onion and garlic in a little oil until soft. Stir in the meat and cook until browned. Chop in a food processor. Return to the pan, add the tomato purée, chopped tomato, herbs, flour and stock. Bring to the boil and simmer for 45 minutes. Fry the aubergine slices in a little oil until golden. Pat dry with kitchen paper. Chop in the food processor. Sauté the mushrooms in a little more oil and add to the sauce with the aubergine.

Chicken Pasta Sauce

Serve with tagliatelle (40 g/1½ oz cooked pasta per serving).

MAKES 3 PORTIONS OF SAUCE

1 boneless chicken breast, skinned
a little margarine, melted
5 cm/2 inches white of leek, sliced

3 tomatoes, skinned, seeded and
chopped

Baste the chicken breast with a little melted margarine and grill for 20 minutes or sauté the chicken for about 10 minutes.
   Sauté the leek in a little margarine for 5 minutes. Add the chopped tomato and continue to cook for 2–3 minutes. Chop the chicken finely and combine it with the vegetables and cooked pasta or purée if necessary.

Tomato and Cheese Pasta Sauce

Delicious poured over pasta and steamed vegetables. Serve
25 g/1 oz cooked pasta and 50 g/2 oz vegetables per portion.

MAKES 3 PORTIONS OF SAUCE

1 small onion, finely chopped
vegetable oil
3 medium tomatoes, skinned, seeded
and chopped

50 g/2 oz curd cheese
40 g/1½ oz Cheddar cheese, grated
50 ml/2 fl oz milk

Sauté the onion in a little oil until transparent, then add the
tomatoes and continue to cook for 2–3 minutes. Stir in the cheeses
and milk until the sauce has thickened. Put through a mouli to make a
smooth sauce.

Pour the sauce over the pasta and vegetables (which can be roughly
chopped if necessary).

Mushroom, Tomato and Courgette
Pasta Sauce

Choose pasta shapes which are easy for your baby to pick up with
his fingers. The creamy mushroom sauce will stick to the pasta. If
your baby prefers to be spoon-fed, choose very small pasta shapes
or chop the pasta into small pieces.

MAKES 4 PORTIONS OF SAUCE

25 g/1 oz margarine
1 tablespoon plain flour
175 ml/6 fl oz milk
100 g/4 oz button mushrooms,
washed and sliced

2 courgettes, washed and sliced
2 medium tomatoes, skinned, seeded
and chopped
1 teaspoon chopped basil

To make the creamy sauce, use half the margarine, the flour and the milk and make in the usual way (see page 59). Sauté the mushrooms in half the remaining margarine for 2 minutes. Mix them together with the white sauce and purée in a blender.

Steam the courgettes until tender (about 20 minutes). Sauté the tomatoes together with the basil in the remaining margarine for 1 minute.

Pour the mushroom sauce over cooked pasta and stir in the tomatoes and courgettes. ☺ ☹

Pasta Shell Salad

This can be made with all sorts of different pasta – animal-shaped pasta is fun if you can find it! You can vary the basic recipe by adding different vegetables like sweetcorn or red pepper. Toast the sesame seeds in a dry frying pan until golden.

MAKES 3 PORTIONS

CHICKEN SALAD	FISH SALAD
1 cooked chicken breast	*100–175 g/4–6 oz can tuna, or*
1 tomato, skinned, seeded and	*salmon drained*
chopped	*2 tablespoons salad cream or*
¼ cucumber, chopped	*mayonnaise*
1 dessertspoon mayonnaise	*75 g/3 oz sweetcorn*
1 dessertspoon cottage cheese	*1 large tomato, skinned, seeded and*
1 teaspoon tomato ketchup	*chopped*
50 g/2 oz cooked pasta shells	*1 spring onion, very finely chopped*
1 tablespoon toasted sesame seeds	*50 g/2 oz cooked pasta shells*
	2 tablespoons toasted sesame seeds

Choose chicken or fish salad. Mix all the ingredients together except for the sesame seeds which you sprinkle over the top.

☺ ☹

NINE TO TWELVE MONTH MEAL PLANNER

	Breakfast	*Sleep*	*Lunch*
Day 1	Fruity Swiss Muesli Yoghurt with Dried Fruit Milk	Milk	Chicken and Apple Balls Finger vegetables Strawberry Rice Pudding Juice
Day 2	Weetabix Cheese on toast Fruit Milk	Milk	Special Steak Jelly Juice
Day 3	Scrambled egg and toast Fruit with cottage cheese Milk	Milk	Haddock in Orange Sauce Baked Apples with Raisins Juice
Day 4	Cheese and Raisin Delight Cheerios (or other cereal) Fruit Milk	Milk	Liver Casserole Multi-Coloured Casserole Papaya Purée Juice
Day 5	French Toast Fruit Compote Milk	Milk	Bang Bang Chicken Cabbage Surprise Jelly Juice
Day 6	Fruity Swiss Muesli Yoghurt and Dried Fruit Milk	Milk	Beef Casserole with Carrots Baked Bananas Juice
Day 7	Cheese Scramble Fruity Yoghurt Milk	Milk	Chicken with Winter Vegetables Fresh Pear with Semolina Juice

Tea	Dinner	Bedtime
Cabbage Surprise Fruit Milk	Miniature sandwiches Finger vegetables Juice	Milk
Pasta Napolitana Courgette Purée with Cottage Cheese Milk	Fruit with *Petit Suisse* Rusk Juice	Milk
Pasta and vegetables with Tomato and Cheese Sauce Fruit and Yoghurt Jelly Milk	Leek and Potato Purée Fruit Juice	Milk
Plaice with Herbs Apple and Blackberry Milk	Finger vegetables with dip Yoghurt Juice	Milk
Fingers of Sole, cooked vegetables as finger food Strawberry Rice Pudding Milk	Vegetables in Cheese Sauce Fruit Juice	Milk
Popeye Pasta Apple Purée Milk	Gratin of Carrots Fruit and Yoghurt Jelly Juice	Milk
Lentil and Vegetable Purée Cheese Fruit Milk	Pasta with Mushroom, Tomato and Courgette Sauce Apple Purée Rusk; Juice	Milk

CHAPTER FIVE

TODDLERS

I find that beyond the age of one, toddlers prefer to exercise their independence and feed themselves. Let your toddler experiment using a spoon and fork – you never know, some food might find its way into his mouth! A handy tip is to put a clean towel or some kitchen paper under your toddler's high chair to catch the food that gets dropped over the side; this will make sure the food is still clean and can be given back to your child. A 'Pelican' bib – a strong plastic bib which has a tray at the bottom to catch stray food – is also good. If your toddler has difficulty eating with a spoon, try giving him finger foods like goujons of fish or raw vegetables with a dip. You must still be careful, though, to keep food like olives, nuts or fresh lychees out of the reach of young children. Toddlers love to put everything in their mouths and it would be so easy for them to choke on such foods.

Toddlers, unlike adults, do not have strict meal times. They are probably more sensible than us and will eat when they are hungry and no amount of coaxing will get them to eat when they are not. Many toddlers prefer lots of small meals during the day to three main meals. In fact doctors have proved that this is a healthier way of eating. There is plenty of time when he grows older and when he goes to school to establish a regular meal pattern. There is a whole section in this book on healthy snacks, so don't make the mistake of giving your toddler sweets or processed snacks when he could enjoy eating a dip with a bowl of raw vegetables much more. Toddlers who get used to eating healthy snacks are more likely to continue the same habits later on in life. However, it would also be wrong to make sweets and doughnuts the forbidden fruit, or your toddler would crave them all the more and gorge himself on them whenever he was out of the house.

Many toddlers enjoy eating much more sophisticated food than we would imagine possible. Let your child try food from your plate and you may find yourself very surprised by the tastes he enjoys. Of course food from Mummy's or Daddy's plate is much more interesting than his own meal and you can sometimes entice your child to eat better if you put his meal on your plate. But the point at this stage is that the toddler can now eat, to a large extent, what you adults are eating. I am a great believer in giving toddlers 'grown-up' foods as soon as possible and almost all the recipes following are suitable for the whole family. *Do* eat with your child rather than just sit there shovelling food into his mouth. He'll eat much more happily *with* you – after all, who enjoys eating alone?

Try and reform your own eating habits by adding less salt and sugar to your food and your toddler will be able to enjoy almost everything you cook. Happy meal times together, and I hope your children will introduce you to some great new recipes.

My Child Won't Eat!

After the age of one, your child will be expending much more energy and nearly all toddlers at some stage will lose interest in food and would much rather play with their toys and run around. This can be a very difficult time and it is important not to make a big fuss if your child refuses to eat. He will eat when he is hungry and the more you fuss the more he will refuse his food. Be patient with him, he will grow out of this phase.

If your toddler really enjoys his food and eats well at meal times, then you really are a lucky mother. I know so many mothers who worry constantly that their child is not eating enough. Most of these worries are unnecessary and toddlers can thrive very well on remarkably little food.

Toddlers are very unpredictable; some days they will be ravenous, and other days they will eat practically nothing. If you judge a child's food intake over a whole week, you won't worry as much if one day he refuses to eat anything.

Many mothers complain that their toddler will not touch meat or fish but there are lots of other equally good sources of protein like peanut butter, eggs or dairy produce. Then there are the mothers who are tearing their hair out because their children will only eat one thing. This is also quite normal; children, unlike adults, like repetition in their diet and they are often wary of trying new foods. Very often, if you let your child choose his own diet, you would be surprised that he might, without any coaxing on your part, choose a balanced one.

There are several ways in which you can try to encourage your child to eat. You might vary the venue of his meals. My son enjoys eating his meals in the Wendy house in the garden. He also loves to have a little tea party and invite his favourite teddy bears; we lay food on a low table in his playroom, he pretends to feed the bears and then eats the food himself. It is all part of a game and he loves it. Eating becomes fun and is no longer a battle of wills.

Toddlers enjoy playing with food and they are interested in the feel of different foods. It is a good idea sometimes to let your child help prepare his meals; for example, he could help you stir the jelly or shell the peas. This is all part of a learning process and food should be fun. Let your toddler poke his finger into the jelly and see it wobble – there is plenty of time to teach him table manners once he has finished experimenting. You may well stimulate an interest in food by getting him to 'help' (under supervision, of course). My son is always willing to lend a helping hand, especially when it comes to making biscuits; he loves to knead the dough, roll it out and cut it into shapes, much more fun than play dough!

Letting them experiment with different spoons and forks and praising them when they manage to get the food into their mouth is another way to encourage them to eat. We have little Chinese meals at home and I feed them with chopsticks. You should see how they enjoy it and how wide they open their mouths!

A great deal of problem eating can be overcome by attractive presentation. We can learn a lot from the Japanese who believe that food should please the eye as well as the stomach. Colour is very important and it is interesting that most toddlers go for the brightly coloured foods first. Try and choose contrasting colours to make the food look appealing. It is a good idea to use plastic plates with separate compartments (you can buy these in most supermarkets) and present your toddler with two or three foods in separate sections – keep the dessert out of sight until the main course has been eaten!

Sometimes it is fun to arrange food in a pattern on the plate. You can help teach your child by arranging food in the shape of numbers or letters or make the food into the shape of a face. You can use some small-sized novelty biscuit cutters to cut out shapes from bread, sandwiches or cheese to stimulate your child's interest. Another tip is to call food by funny names like Peter Rabbit carrots or Andy Pandy soup. You may laugh but if your toddler thinks this is what his favourite character eats for lunch, he is more likely to eat it himself!

Never put too much food on a plate – much better that he should ask for more. Toddlers love individual portions of food. Make miniature shepherd's pie, for example (much nicer than a dollop of meat and potatoes on a plate) and miniature cakes rather than slices from a large cake.

If you have given your toddler a good choice of foods and he still refuses to eat, it is not then a good idea to offer him the contents of the fridge and larder. Explain that this is his meal and that there is

nothing else on offer. If he is very restless and clearly not interested, just put the food back in the fridge and bring it out a little later. You will be making a rod for your own back otherwise and nine times out of ten he is just not hungry. Adults are conditioned into eating three meals a day but toddlers will only eat when they are hungry – and no child has ever starved to death through stubbornness.

If you make eating fun, then your children will be tucking in with you. Eat as a family as much as possible. An occasional trip to a restaurant does wonders to stimulate a child's appetite. Even just going to a friend's house for tea can help sometimes, especially if there is another child present who likes to tuck in!

The Foods to Choose

Now that your child is twelve months old, you can switch from formula to whole (silver or red-top) cow's milk. Do not give him skimmed milk. Unless he is really obese he will need a diet that contains at least 40 per cent fat; and unless obesity runs in your family, the chances are that you do not need to worry about it. A lot of parents nowadays are concerned about their children's cholesterol level and put them on low-fat diets from a very early age but cholesterol guidelines do not apply in the same way to most normal toddlers as they do to adults. Growing children need more dietary fat than adults and should not be given low-fat produce. Fat is a rich source of both the fatty acids and the fat-soluble vitamins needed for a child's growth. Also fat is concentrated calories and provides almost twice as much energy as either proteins or carbohydrates. There are, of course, exceptions to this rule, and an overweight toddler should have his fat intake restricted. In general terms, stick to healthy cooking, cutting fat from meat, and cooking with vegetable fats rather than animal or saturated fats.

Vegetable dishes at this stage can be served to the whole family as a main meal. This is useful if your child goes through a stage of refusing to eat any meat and you need to supplement his diet with protein-rich foods like nuts, beans, pulses and soya products. (It's also vital for children who are being brought up as vegetarians.)

You can now include healthy 'convenience' fish like canned tuna and

salmon which are cheaper than fresh fish. Chicken dishes too can be more versatile – I've tried to make this a fairly international section. Chicken is so low in fat, and such a favourite with us that I'm sure one day my husband will turn into one, the amount he eats!

Although more and more people are turning away from red meat in favour of fish and chicken, you must bear in mind that red meat provides more iron and zinc than either fish or poultry and that you should supplement your child's diet by providing other sources of these minerals – leafy green vegetables, beans and nuts for instance. You could offer your toddler foods like hamburgers and shepherd's pie, so long as they are lean – you can ask your butcher to mince some lean cuts especially for you. Do not give your toddler processed meats like sausages, salami or corned beef.

Pasta is still a great favourite with toddlers. There is a wonderful variety available to choose from; you can stuff canneloni, make a tomato sauce for fresh ravioli containing Ricotta and spinach, or entice your child to eat meat by making spaghetti bolognese. (My son, Nicholas, who shows little enthusiasm for eating minced meat, will gobble it all up if it is stuffed inside canneloni or served as a spaghetti sauce.) You can even teach your toddler to read by buying alphabet spaghetti! Individual pieces of pasta like penne (tubes) or papardelle (bow-ties) are still much easier for toddlers to eat than long strands of spaghetti. (Although Nicholas, when 20 months, invented his own method of eating spaghetti – he held it out in front of him by the two ends and sucked in from the middle! Not the height of good manners perhaps, but certainly very efficient.)

FRUIT AND DESSERTS

There are many recipes here for cold and cooked desserts which can be enjoyed by the whole family, but there is still nothing more delicious or better for you and your child than fresh ripe fruit. None of the vitamins and nutrients are destroyed through cooking, and it makes great finger food for your toddler. My son adores fruit so much that we have to hide the fruit bowl until he finishes his main course. He would far rather eat fruit than sickly sweet puddings and chocolates. Serve fruit on a daily basis and one of these desserts every now and again as a treat.

Present fresh fruit in an attractive way; contrast colours on the plate; cut the fruits into interesting shapes and arrange in patterns. Always make sure that you remove any stones before giving to your toddler – he could so easily choke.

Where raw fruit is concerned, there are endless variations on a theme. Purée or grate fruits and mix them with cottage cheese or yoghurt and wheatgerm. Cut the fruit into bite-sized chunks and cover with yoghurt and honey or home-made custard. Dried fruits which have been soaked make great finger foods.

Try giving your children some more exotic fruits like Sharon fruit which looks like an orange tomato and is grown in Israel. It tastes wonderful mashed with cottage cheese and can be found in large supermarkets when it is in season. Kiwi fruit is high in Vitamin C and makes a good snack cut into slices and mango and papaya blend very well with dairy produce.

Fruits can also be puréed for use in ice creams. Ice creams in all colours, shapes and sizes are sold all over the world.

However the quality of some products has nothing to do with the true home-made experience. I think that there is nothing to beat the combination of milk, cream or yoghurt and wonderful home-made fruit purées – far better for all of us than ingredients like skimmed milk, vegetable fat, glucose syrup, whey solids, guar gum, emulsifier (E471), stabilisers and artificial flavours that can be found in many commercial ice creams lingering in the deep freezes of supermarkets. In Britain alone, on average £400 million pounds a year is spent on ice cream and there *are* some good commercial ice creams made from natural ingredients only but you do need to look out for them.

If you enjoy making your own ice cream it really is worth investing in a small ice-cream making machine. Believe me, you will put it to good use through the year and your children will be very popular with their friends when they come round for tea. If you do not have an ice-cream maker do not be put off making your own home-made ice creams. Just pour the prepared mixture into a plastic container, cover with foil or a polythene bag and place in the freezer until firm (3– 4 hours). Break the mixture into pieces, put it into a food processor bowl and beat with a metal blade until light and fluffy but not thawed. This should get rid of the ice particles in the mixture, and for a really smooth texture, it is advisable to repeat this process at least twice during

freezing. Put the ice cream back into the freezer in the plastic container. Ice cream tastes best if you take it out of the freezer 10 minutes before you serve it.

Another simple way of serving ice cream is to pour the mixture into ice-lolly moulds – toddlers love these (see page 171).

BAKING FOR TODDLERS

A toddler's first birthday is a big occasion in his life and probably even more exciting for his parents and grandparents! It is great fun preparing the food for a child's party. Anyone can go to a shop and order a birthday cake in the shape of a train, but how much more impressive and satisfying it is to bake and decorate your own. Your child will love to help with the mixing and decorating – probably more fun than eating it.

Any basic sponge or fruit cake mixture could be adapted to a novelty shape, if you like. There are many smaller cakes which can be served at a child's tea party. Many of the baking recipes contain healthy ingredients, cutting out undesirables as much as possible but some are sheer uncompromised treats.

HEALTHY SNACKS

If your toddler is happy to eat three main meals a day, then that is wonderful and very convenient for everyone, but let's face it, nearly all toddlers snack between meals. Whereas for some this just supplements their meal, many toddlers do not have the patience to sit down and eat a proper meal and they get most of their nutrition from snacks during the day. Toddlers' stomachs are small and it is often difficult for them to eat enough at breakfast, say, to last them until lunchtime when they have been rushing around all morning. As I said earlier, lots of small meals – healthy snacks – during the day are in fact healthier than three main meals. Snacks are therefore a very important part of a toddler's diet. If you encourage your child when he is very young to enjoy eating healthy snacks in preference to sweets and crisps, it is likely that he will continue these habits later in life and enjoy a much healthier diet.

Keep your larder and fridge full of healthy snacks and when you take your toddler out, try to remember to take a small bag of healthy snacks with you. Toddlers expend a lot of energy and it doesn't take them long to get hungry again after a meal.

Textures and Quantities

There is no longer any need to purée your child's food; on the contrary, he should be getting used to chewing. The longer you continue with purées because that is the way your child prefers his food, the more difficult it will become to encourage him to chew and swallow his food properly. In fact chewing on something hard like a raw carrot should help to relieve sore gums. A lot of toddlers, however, do not like to chew chunks of meat, and it is sometimes necessary to break meat down in a blender before serving. I find that minced meat, liver or chicken goes down better with most toddlers than chunks of meat.

Underneath each recipe, I have given quantities in adult portions. Every child is different, and you must gauge the portion size on your toddler's appetite. He can eat anything from one-quarter of an adult portion to a whole portion if he is exceptionally hungry and greedy! (If your toddler is becoming overweight, then you should consult your doctor and consider putting him on a low-fat diet.)

VEGETABLES

Ratatouille

Vegetables tend to be quite soft in ratatouille and so are easy for your toddler to chew. Choose firm aubergines and courgettes; if they are not fresh, the ratatouille may taste bitter. For a more substantial meal finish the dish with a cheesy crumble topping.

MAKES 6 ADULT PORTIONS

2 aubergines
salt and pepper to taste
2 onions, peeled and chopped
1/2 clove of garlic, crushed (optional)
olive oil
1 green and 1 red sweet pepper,
seeded and diced

4 courgettes, trimmed and sliced
2 large tomatoes, skinned, seeded and
chopped
1 bay leaf
1 sprig of thyme
1 tablespoon chopped parsley

Cut the aubergines into 5 mm/¼ inch slices (do not peel). Put them in a colander, sprinkle with salt and set aside for 30–40 minutes (to drain out bitter flavours). Meanwhile cook the onion and garlic in 2 tablespoons of the oil until the onion is soft and transparent. Add the sweet peppers and a little more oil if necessary and cook for a further 3 minutes. Transfer the onions and peppers to a casserole.

Rinse the aubergines and dry with kitchen paper. Fry them in very hot olive oil to begin with (to seal the surface), then reduce the heat and fry for a further 5 minutes. Drain. Transfer the aubergines to the casserole and add the sliced courgettes, chopped tomato, herbs and seasoning to taste. Cook in an oven preheated to 350°F(180°C)Gas 4, covered, for about 30 minutes.

Special Fried Rice

Babies love rice and this is very appealing as it is so colourful. For older children you can make little sailing boats. Cut a cooked red pepper in half, stuff each half with rice and stick two corn chips upright in the rice to look like sails.

MAKES 6 ADULT PORTIONS

225 g/8 oz basmati rice
1 small onion, finely chopped
75 g/3 oz carrots, washed, scrubbed and diced
25 g/1 oz margarine or butter

175 g/6 oz frozen peas
75 g/3 oz sweet red or yellow pepper, washed and diced
2 tablespoons sesame oil
2 chopped hard-boiled eggs

Wash the rice thoroughly and cook for 15 to 20 minutes until soft. Sauté the onion until transparent, add the carrot and sauté for 3 minutes. Add the peas and peppers and cook for 3 minutes more. Heat the sesame oil in a frying pan, fry the rice for 2 to 3 minutes. Add the vegetables and egg.

Stuffed Potatoes

Stuffed potatoes make an excellent meal for toddlers and there are endless variations on the fillings you can make. Prick medium potatoes all over and brush with oil. Bake in an oven preheated to 375°F(190°C)Gas 5 for 1¼–1½ hours, or until tender (or you can bake them in the microwave). Carefully spoon the soft flesh out of the skins leaving enough round the sides so that the skins keep their shape. You are now ready to make the various fillings.

Vegetable and Cheese Potato Filling

MAKES 4 ADULT PORTIONS

25 g/1 oz each of small broccoli and cauliflower florets
4 medium baked potatoes
15 g/½ oz margarine
120 ml/4 fl oz milk

50 g/2 oz grated Cheddar cheese
2 medium tomatoes, skinned and cut into small pieces
½ teaspoon salt
grated cheese to finish

Steam the cauliflower and broccoli until they are tender (about 6 minutes), then chop finely. Meanwhile mash the potato flesh with the margarine and milk until smooth and creamy. Mix in the cheese, tomatoes, cooked chopped vegetables and salt and scoop the mixture back into the potato skins. Sprinkle a little extra grated cheese on top and brown under the grill.

Chicken or Tuna Potato Filling

MAKES 2 ADULT PORTIONS

*1 medium onion, peeled and finely
chopped
1 tablespoon cooking oil
50 g/2 oz button mushrooms, washed
and thinly sliced
2 medium baked potatoes*

*15 g/½ oz margarine
120 ml/4 fl oz milk
175 g/6 oz cooked chicken breast,
chopped, or canned tuna, drained and
flaked
2 tablespoons chopped parsley
1 tablespoon tomato ketchup*

Sauté the onion in the oil until transparent. Add the mushrooms and cook for a further 3 minutes. Mash the potato flesh with the margarine and milk, then combine with all the remaining ingredients. Spoon into the potato skins. Bake for 10 minutes in an oven preheated to 350°F(180°C)Gas 4 and serve.

Stuffed Tomatoes

Another easy dish, which can be prepared in advance and which
looks very appealing.

MAKES 2 ADULT PORTIONS

2 eggs
2 medium tomatoes
1 tablespoon mayonnaise

1 tablespoon snipped chives
salt and pepper

Hard-boil both the eggs. Meanwhile skin the tomatoes, then cut
the tops off and scoop out the inside. Discard the seeds but keep
the tiny bits of flesh. When the eggs are ready, peel and mash them
together with the pieces of tomato, mayonnaise, chives and a little salt
and pepper. Stuff into the tomatoes and replace the tomato tops on
the egg mixture.

☺ ☹

Tasty Peanut Rissoles

Combining vegetables with nuts makes a good high-protein meal
for your toddler and this is a delicious combination which the rest
of the family will enjoy too!

MAKES 8 RISSOLES

1 onion, peeled and finely chopped
1 celery stalk, diced
1 carrot, scraped and diced
vegetable oil
1/2 sweet red pepper, seeded and diced
*50 g/2 oz mushrooms, washed and
diced*

50 g/2 oz green beans
50 g/2 oz unsalted roasted peanuts
50 g/2 oz cooked brown rice
1 egg, beaten
salt and freshly ground pepper
*3 slices brown bread made into
breadcrumbs*

Fry the onion, celery and carrot in a little oil for 3 minutes, then add the red pepper and mushrooms and continue to fry until soft. Drain off any excess fat.

Meanwhile steam the green beans until tender, about 8–10 minutes. Chop the nuts and beans in a food processor and add these to the rest of the cooked vegetables along with the rice. Stir in enough beaten egg to moisten, a little seasoning and a third of the bread-crumbs and mix well.

Form the mixture into flat round rissoles and roll them in the remaining breadcrumbs. Put the rissoles in the fridge to harden for 1 hour. When you are ready to eat, shallow-fry the rissoles in hot oil.

Potato, Courgette and Cheese Fritters

These crispy vegetable fritters have a delicious taste.

MAKES 4 ADULT PORTIONS

2 medium potatoes, peeled
2 medium courgettes, trimmed
50 g/2 oz Cheddar cheese, grated
2 eggs, lightly beaten

a pinch of ground nutmeg
salt and pepper to taste
2 tablespoons vegetable oil
25 g/1 oz margarine

Coarsely grate the potatoes and courgettes, then get rid of as much of their liquid as possible by squeezing them between two plates. Put the vegetables in a bowl and add the grated cheese, eggs and seasonings.

Heat the oil and margarine in a frying pan. Form the vegetable mixture into round, flat cakes and cook over a medium heat, turning frequently to brown both sides.

Spanish Omelette

This is good served cold and cut into wedges the next day. I give suggestions on the right for additions to the basic omelette.

MAKES 6 ADULT PORTIONS

2 medium potatoes, peeled and diced
cooking or olive oil
1 onion, peeled and finely chopped
3 tablespoons chopped green and red
sweet pepper
50 g/2 oz button mushrooms, washed
and sliced
1 tablespoon chopped parsley
1 tablespoon grated Parmesan cheese
salt and pepper
4 eggs

Suggested variations
1 tablespoon grated Gruyère
OR
1 large chopped tomato
1 tablespoon tomato ketchup
OR
50 g/2 oz peas
1 tablespoon snipped chives
OR
50 g/2 oz drained canned tuna
250 g/9 oz drained canned chopped
tomato
OR
100 g/4 oz cooked ham or bacon,
cubed

Fry the diced potato in a little oil until brown. Drain well. Fry the onion. After a few minutes, add the peppers. When the onions have turned golden brown, add the mushroom and parsley and cook, stirring over a medium heat, for about 3 minutes. In a bowl, combine the onion mixture with the potatoes, Parmesan, any variation ingredients and season to taste. Beat the eggs and pour them over the vegetable mixture. Heat 2 tablespoons of oil in a frying pan and tip the pan to coat half-way up the sides. Fry the egg mixture for about 8–10 minutes (or until the omelette is lightly browned underneath). To finish, brown under a hot grill for about 3 minutes. Cut into wedges. Serve hot or cold.

☺ ☹

Vegetarian Rissoles

These rissoles can be eaten hot or cold. They make a great meal for the whole family served with a fresh salad. They freeze very well. It is best to freeze them just after they are rolled in breadcrumbs, then you can fry them just before serving.

MAKES 8 RISSOLES

1 onion, peeled and finely chopped
50 g/2 oz white of leek, chopped
vegetable oil
175 g/6 oz cauliflower, broken into florets
175 g/6 oz cabbage, shredded
175 g/6 oz courgettes, trimmed and sliced
salt and pepper to taste

225 g/8 oz mushrooms, washed and finely chopped
a squeeze of lemon juice
50 g/2 oz plain flour
2 teaspoons Marmite, melted in 50 ml/2 fl oz hot water
6 slices wholemeal or granary bread, made into breadcrumbs
1 egg, beaten

Fry the chopped onion and leek in a little oil until transparent. Cook the cauliflower, cabbage and courgette until tender (preferably in a steamer) with a little salt to taste. When the onions are cooked, stir in the chopped mushrooms and cook for a further 3 minutes. Add the lemon juice. Roughly chop the cooked cauliflower, cabbage and courgettes and add to the mushrooms and onions. Stir in the flour and mix well. Stir in the Marmite water and a little salt and pepper to taste. Stir in a few of the breadcrumbs to thicken the mixture, and make into small rissoles with floured hands. (It is best to leave the mixture to cool down first!) Dip the rissoles into beaten egg, a little extra flour and then into the breadcrumbs. Chill for 30 minutes to firm up before cooking. Fry in hot oil until golden and crisp on both sides.

Vegetable Salad with Raspberry Vinegar

This is a refreshing salad for a summer's lunch. The dressing complements the nutty flavour of the sweetcorn and adds a little sweetness to the salad.

MAKES 4 ADULT PORTIONS

100 g/4 oz cauliflower, broken into small florets
100 g/4 oz French beans
175 g/6 oz frozen sweetcorn
sugar to taste
¼ small lettuce, shredded

8 cherry tomatoes, cut in half
1 hard-boiled egg, grated

Dressing
1 tablespoon raspberry vinegar
2 tablespoons hazelnut oil
salt and pepper to taste

Steam the cauliflower and beans until tender (about 15 minutes). Cook the frozen sweetcorn for about 4 minutes in boiling water with a little sugar and salt. When the cauliflower, beans and sweetcorn have cooled, put all the salad ingredients in a bowl with the grated egg sprinkled on top. Mix the dressing together with a fork and pour it over the salad.

☺ ☹

Spinach with Sesame Sauce

This dish originates from Japan. It is very nutritious, simple to prepare and delicious. In Japanese restaurants, it is served cold, but it can also be served hot.

MAKES 2 ADULT PORTIONS

25 g/1 oz sesame seeds
225 g/8 oz spinach, carefully washed and tough stalks removed

1 tablespoon soy sauce
1 teaspoon sugar
3 tablespoons apple juice

Sprinkle the sesame seeds into a dry pan, cover and heat, shaking constantly until a pale golden. Meanwhile cook the spinach in a small amount of water for 3 to 4 minutes. When the spinach is cooked press out any water by squeezing between two plates. Crush the seeds in a mouli (reserving a few to sprinkle over the spinach) and they will become a fine powder. Mix the powder with the soy sauce, sugar and juice until it has the consistency of cream. Roughly chop the spinach, pour over the sesame sauce and sprinkle with the toasted whole sesame seeds.

Baked Bean Pie with Spinach and Potato

Baked beans are a great favourite with children and this is a delicious way of making them into a whole meal.

MAKES 5 ADULT PORTIONS

400 g/14 oz can baked beans

Spinach cheese sauce
350 g/12 oz frozen chopped spinach
7 g/¼ oz margarine
1 dessertspoon plain flour
120 ml/4 fl oz milk
25 g/1 oz Parmesan cheese, grated

Topping
2 large potatoes, peeled and chopped
50 ml/2 fl oz milk
15 g/½ oz margarine

For the topping, boil the potatoes for about 20 minutes or until soft. Drain.

Meanwhile, for the sauce, cook the frozen spinach over a low heat until cooked through. Drain well. Use the margarine, flour and milk to make a thick white sauce (see page 59). Take the saucepan off the heat and stir in the grated Parmesan cheese. Mix the cheese sauce with the cooked spinach. Mash the cooked potatoes together with the milk and half the margarine.

Put the spinach sauce into a suitably sized ovenproof dish. Cover with the baked beans and spread the mashed potato on top. Bake in an oven preheated to 350°F(180°C)Gas 4 for 10–15 minutes, then dot the potato with the remaining margarine. Finish with 5 minutes under a hot grill to make a crispy topping.

FISH

Grandma's Gefilte Fish

This is my mother's traditional recipe. It is very appealing to children because of the slightly sweet taste of the balls. My son, Nicholas, loves them and they are very easy for him to hold and eat himself. Adults can eat them with horseradish sauce.

MAKES ABOUT 20 BALLS

450 g/1 lb minced fish fillet (mix any of the following: haddock, bream, whiting, cod or hake)
1 egg, beaten

1 onion, peeled and chopped very finely in the food processor
2 dessertspoons sugar
salt and pepper to taste
light cooking oil

Mix all the ingredients well (except for the oil), and shape into golf-ball-sized balls. Fry carefully until golden brown all over. Drain on kitchen paper. Serve hot or cold.

Boiled Minced Fish Balls

These are best served cold.

MAKES 20 BALLS

*450 g/1 lb minced fish (see previous
page)
1 egg, beaten
1 carrot, peeled and grated
1 tablespoon chopped parsley
1 onion, peeled and chopped very
finely in the food processor
salt and pepper to taste
2 dessertspoons sugar*

*Fish stock
Some fish bones
1 medium onion, peeled and sliced
2 carrots, scraped and sliced
1 bay leaf
sprig of parsley
4 peppercorns
a little sugar*

For the stock, put the fish bones, onion, carrots, bay leaf, parsley, peppercorns, a little salt and a little sugar into a saucepan with 900 ml/1½ pints water. Bring to the boil, skim, and then simmer for 1 hour. Remove the fish bones from the stock.

Mix all the ingredients for the fish balls together. Form into small balls using wet hands. Place the fish into the boiling stock and simmer for about 1 hour.

Nursery Fish Pie

A good, old-fashioned favourite.

MAKES 3 ADULT PORTIONS

350 g/12 oz cod fillet
150 ml/5 fl oz milk
½ bay leaf
salt and pepper (optional)
25 g/1 oz margarine
15 g/½ oz plain flour
2 tablespoons grated Cheddar cheese
1 tablespoon chopped parsley
1 hard-boiled egg, chopped
a squeeze of lemon juice

Topping
350 g/12 oz potatoes, peeled and cut
into pieces
1 tablespoon milk
15 g/½ oz margarine

Cut the fish into pieces, put into a saucepan with the milk, bay leaf and a little light seasoning. Bring to the boil, then simmer, uncovered, for about 10 minutes. While the fish is cooking, cook the potato for the topping in boiling salted water until soft. Drain well, mash with the milk and margarine and lightly season.

Drain the fish, reserving the cooking liquid and carefully remove any skin and bones. Melt half the margarine in a heavy-bottomed saucepan and add the flour. Cook gently for 1 minute, then add the fish liquid gradually, then bring to the boil, stirring. Simmer the sauce for 3–4 minutes, stirring continuously until smooth. Take off the heat, add the grated cheese and continue to stir until it has completely melted. Fold in the fish, parsley and boiled egg. Add a little seasoning and a squeeze of lemon. Place the fish in a greased serving dish and top with the mashed potato. Bake in an oven preheated to 350°F(180°C)Gas 4 for 15–20 minutes then dot with the remaining margarine and grill for about 2 minutes until brown and crispy.

Fish in Creamy Mushroom Sauce

For older children, cook 225 g/8 oz fresh spinach and lay each whole fillet on a bed of spinach and pour over the sauce.

MAKES 4 ADULT PORTIONS

1 small onion, peeled and finely chopped
25 g/1 oz margarine
225 g/8 oz button mushrooms, washed and finely chopped

2 tablespoons lemon juice
2 tablespoons chopped parsley
2 tablespoons plain flour
300 ml/10 fl oz milk
1 sole (or plaice), filleted

Fry the onion in half the margarine until transparent. Add the mushrooms, lemon juice and parsley and cook for 2 minutes. Add the flour and cook for 2 minutes, stirring constantly. Add the milk gradually and cook, stirring constantly until the sauce is thick and smooth.

Fry the sole fillets in the rest of the margarine for 2–3 minutes on each side. Cut or flake the fish into small pieces and mix with the mushroom sauce. Alternatively, cover the fish with the mushroom sauce and bake in the oven preheated to 350°F(180°C)Gas 4 for about 15 minutes or until the fish just flakes.

Gratin of Sole

A very tasty fish recipe which is so easy to make.

MAKES 4 ADULT PORTIONS

4 fillets of lemon sole
salt and pepper to taste
¹/₂ small lemon
100 g/4 oz wholemeal breadcrumbs

50 g/2 oz Cheddar cheese, grated
1 heaped tablespoon chopped parsley
50 g/2 oz margarine, melted

Lay the fillets in a greased ovenproof dish and season with salt, pepper and lemon juice. Put the breadcrumbs, cheese and parsley in a bowl and stir in the melted margarine. Put the breadcrumb mixture on top of the fish in the dish. Place the fish under a preheated grill for about 8 minutes until the breadcrumbs have turned a golden brown and the fish is cooked.

Sole with Tomatoes and Mushrooms

This looks very attractive with the fillets rolled up and covered with a pink sauce. For a more filling meal, lay the fish on top of baked potatoes cut in half, scooped out and re-filled with buttered mashed potato.

MAKES 4 ADULT PORTIONS

1 medium onion, peeled and chopped
25 g/1 oz margarine
2 medium tomatoes, skinned, seeded and diced
225 g/8 oz mushrooms, washed and sliced

4 fillets of sole
salt and pepper
1 tablespoon tomato ketchup
2 tablespoons double cream

Sauté the onion in the margarine until soft. Add the tomato and mushrooms and cook for 2–3 minutes. Season the fish with salt and pepper, roll up and secure with a wooden toothpick. Place the fish in a greased dish, spoon over the tomato sauce and dot with the ketchup. Cook, uncovered, for 15 minutes in an oven preheated to 400°F(200°C)Gas 6. Remove the fish fillets and liquidise the sauce in a blender. Stir in the cream, then pour over the fish. Serve with mashed potatoes or rice.

Sesame Fish

This is a very quick, easy and tasty fish recipe.

MAKES 2 ADULT PORTIONS

2 fillets of plaice or sole
15 g/¹/₂ oz margarine
1 dessertspoon sesame seeds

1 dessertspoon finely chopped spring onions
a squeeze of lemon juice

Fry the fish fillets in margarine with the sesame seeds and spring onions. Cook over a low heat for 3–4 minutes, turning half-way through. Add a squeeze of lemon juice. Cut fish into small pieces.

Scrambled Fish

Vary by adding chopped tomato or grated cheese before cooking.

MAKES 2 ADULT PORTIONS

100 g/4 oz fillet of haddock
2 tablespoons milk
salt and pepper to taste
25 g/1 oz margarine

1 egg
1 dessertspoon snipped chives
2 slices wholemeal bread, toasted and buttered

Cook the fish with half the milk, seasoning and a tiny piece of the margarine (about 4 minutes in the microwave on High or the same in a pan on top of the stove). Beat the egg, season with salt and pepper and stir in the chives. Add the flaked fish and remaining milk to the egg. Melt the remaining margarine in a saucepan, stir in the fish mixture and cook over a gentle heat for 2 or 3 minutes until it thickens, in the normal way. Serve on hot buttered toast.

Grandma's Tasty Fish Pie

This is one of my mother's recipes which is a great favourite with all the family. There is never any left the next day.

MAKES 6 ADULT PORTIONS

450 g/1 lb skinned fillets of haddock
plain flour
salt and pepper
1 egg, beaten
2 slices brown bread or crisp roll,
made into breadcrumbs
cooking oil
1 onion, peeled and finely chopped
1 red and 1 green sweet pepper,
seeded and chopped

400 g/14 oz can tomatoes, or 2
tablespoons tomato purée

Cheese sauce
25 g/1 oz margarine
1 tablespoon plain flour
250 ml/8 fl oz milk
150 g/5 oz Cheddar cheese, grated
40 g/1¹/₂ Parmesan, grated

Dip the haddock fillets into seasoned flour then into the egg and finally coat in breadcrumbs. Fry in oil until golden brown on both sides. Drain off oil on kitchen paper, then flake the fish into small pieces and place in an ovenproof dish.

Sauté the onion in a very little oil in a frying pan for 3–4 minutes. Add the peppers and continue to cook until soft. Drain the can of tomatoes, chop the tomatoes and add to the peppers and onion. Cook for a further 3–4 minutes then season. Pour over the fish.

Make a cheese sauce with the margarine, flour and milk, stirring over a low heat until smooth and thick (see page 59). Take the saucepan off the heat and stir in 90 g/3¹/₂ oz of the grated cheese, reserving the rest to sprinkle over the top of the fish pie.

Cover the flaked fish and tomato with the cheese sauce and top with the reserved grated Cheddar and Parmesan. Cook in an oven preheated to 350°F(180°C)Gas 4 for 20 minutes. Brown under the grill.

Kedgeree

I am surprised how many toddlers like the taste of smoked fish. Both my children love smoked fish. Smoked fish is very salty, however and can make your toddler very thirsty.

MAKES 4 ADULT PORTIONS

225 g/8 oz smoked haddock (or canned salmon)
75 g/3 oz brown rice
25 g/1 oz margarine
½ small onion, peeled and finely chopped

1 teaspoon tomato ketchup
½ teaspoon curry powder (optional)
1 hard-boiled egg, chopped
1 teaspoon lemon juice
1 tablespoon chopped parsley

Poach the haddock in enough water to cover for 10 minutes or until cooked. Drain, reserving the cooking liquid. Flake the fish carefully, discarding the skin and bones. Cook the rice in the reserved liquid, adding a little extra water if necessary (about 15 minutes).

Melt the margarine in a saucepan and fry the chopped onion until soft but not brown. Stir in the tomato ketchup and curry powder (if used), then add all the rest of the ingredients and cook over a moderate heat for about 5 minutes.

☺ ☹

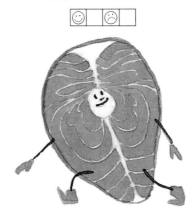

Tuna Bake with Potato Crisps

What child doesn't like potato crisps – here is a nutritious way of making them into a meal.

MAKES 4 ADULT PORTIONS

15 g/¹/₂ oz margarine
1 level tablespoon plain flour
250 ml/8 fl oz milk
1 small can tuna in oil (100–175 g/
4–6 oz), drained and flaked

50 g/2 oz button mushrooms, washed,
sliced and sautéed in a little butter
1 hard-boiled egg, chopped (optional)
pepper
1 bag potato crisps, crushed

Make a white sauce with the margarine, flour and milk (see page 59). Stir constantly, until the sauce thickens. Add the flaked tuna to this, together with the sliced mushrooms, chopped egg and a little seasoning. Add half the crushed crisps and pour this mixture into a greased casserole. Sprinkle the remainder of the crisps on top and bake in the oven preheated to 350°F(180°C)Gas 4 for 30 minutes.

Tuna Tagliatelle

This is my favourite tuna recipe.

MAKES 6 ADULT PORTIONS

¹/₂ onion, peeled and finely chopped
25 g/1 oz margarine
450 ml/15 fl oz can cream of tomato
soup
1 teaspoon cornflour
100–175 g/4–6 oz can tuna, drained
and flaked
a pinch of mixed herbs
1 tablespoon chopped parsley
175 g/6 oz green tagliatelle
grated Parmesan cheese

Mushroom cheese sauce
¹/₂ onion, peeled and finely chopped
50 g/2 oz margarine
50 g/2 oz mushrooms, washed and
sliced
2 tablespoons plain flour
300 ml/10 fl oz milk
100 g/4 oz Cheddar cheese, grated

For the sauce, fry the onion in the margarine until transparent then add the sliced mushrooms and sauté for about 3 minutes. Add the flour and continue stirring the mixture all the time. When it is well mixed, add the milk gradually and cook, stirring until smooth. Remove from the heat and stir in the grated cheese.

Fry the onion in the margarine until soft and stir in the tomato soup which has been thickened with the cornflour mixed with a little cold water. Add the tuna, mixed herbs and chopped parsley.

Boil the tagliatelle in water until *al dente*, then drain. Grease a serving dish and add the tuna and tomato mixed with the noodles and then the mushroom cheese sauce. Top with grated Parmesan. Bake in an oven preheated to 350°F (180°C) Gas 4 for 20 minutes. Brown under a hot grill before serving.

Tuna or Salmon Gratin

If you keep a can of tuna or salmon in the larder, then it is easy to combine it with some leftover vegetables to make a tasty fish pie. The ingredients can be varied according to what you have available.

MAKES 5 ADULT PORTIONS

*100 g/4 oz button mushrooms,
washed and sliced
15 g/½ oz margarine
100 g/4 oz frozen peas
100–175 g/4–6 oz can tuna or
salmon
1 large tomato, skinned, seeded and
cut into chunks
1 hard-boiled egg, chopped*

Sauce
*15 g/½ oz margarine
1 tablespoon plain flour
150 ml/5 fl oz milk
50 g/2 oz Cheddar cheese, grated*

Topping
*2 potatoes, peeled, boiled and mashed
with a little milk, margarine, salt
and pepper
25 g/1 oz Cheddar cheese, grated*

Fry the mushrooms in a little margarine for a couple of minutes, and cook the frozen peas until just tender. Make the sauce in the usual way, with the margarine, flour and milk, stirring over a gentle heat until it thickens (see page 59). Remove from the heat and stir in the grated cheese. Add the tuna or salmon, peas, mushrooms, tomato and chopped egg to the sauce. Pour this mixture into a greased ovenproof dish. Cover with mashed potato and top with grated cheese. Cook for 20 minutes in an oven preheated to 350°F(180°C)Gas 4 and brown under the grill for a couple of minutes before serving.

CHICKEN

Chicken Casserole with Tomatoes and Peppers

An easy-to-make chicken casserole which is delicious served with rice or mashed potato.

MAKES 6 ADULT PORTIONS

6 chicken breasts, on the bone and skinned
plain flour
salt and pepper
cooking oil
2 onions, peeled and finely sliced
2 sweet peppers (1 red, 1 green or 1 yellow), seeded and finely sliced

800 g/28 oz can of tomatoes
2 chicken stock cubes, dissolved in 175 ml/6 fl oz water
1 tablespoon each of chopped parsley and mixed herbs
1 bay leaf
450 g/1 lb button mushrooms, carefully washed

Roll the chicken breasts in seasoned flour and fry them, turning frequently, in a little oil until golden. Meanwhile fry the onion for 3–4 minutes in a little oil until soft, then add the chopped peppers and continue to fry for another 3 minutes. Pat off any excess fat from the cooked chicken with some kitchen paper and drain off excess oil from the pepper and onion.

Drain off the tomato juice and chop the tomatoes into pieces. Put the chicken into a large casserole together with the onion, pepper, tomato, concentrated chicken cube stock, herbs and some seasoning. Cook in an oven preheated to 350°F(180°C)Gas 4 for 30 minutes. Add the button mushrooms and continue to cook for a further 30 minutes.

Bar-B-Q Chicken

Chicken cooked in this way is slightly sweet and very succulent. It is a great favourite with my son. I use a Weber Bar-B-Q, which has a cover, thus enabling me to barbecue food all the year round, even in England.

MAKES 4–5 ADULT PORTIONS

900 g/2 lb breast of chicken, on the bone and skinned

Marinade
3 tablespoons red wine vinegar
1 tablespoon soy sauce
³/₄ tablespoon Worcestershire sauce
¹/₂ tablespoon runny honey
black pepper

Mix all the marinade ingredients together and marinate the chicken for not less than 2 hours. Barbecue the chicken by whichever method you have available, basting the chicken frequently with the sauce (about 35–40 minutes). When cooked, take the chicken off the bone and cut into pieces.

Chicken Satay

These barbecued chicken skewers are fun to eat and very popular with toddlers. Help your child take the meat off the skewers, then remove the skewers – they could become dangerous in the hands of exuberant toddlers.

MAKES ABOUT 4 ADULT PORTIONS

4 chicken breasts, off the bone and skinned
¹/₂ onion, peeled
¹/₂ red sweet pepper, seeded
8 button mushrooms, washed

Marinade
50 ml/2 fl oz light sesame oil
2 tablespoons lemon juice
1 tablespoon smooth peanut butter
3 tablespoons runny honey

In a bowl mix together all the ingredients for the marinade. Cut the chicken, onion and pepper into chunks. Leave the chicken in the marinade for at least 2 hours. Thread the chicken, onion, pepper and mushrooms on to skewers and barbecue basting the chicken frequently with the marinade.

146

Chicken Paprika

This dish is not very spicy so don't be afraid to give it to young children. If you want to make it 'hot' for adults, substitute 1 teaspoon cayenne pepper for paprika. Serve with noodles or rice.

MAKES 4 ADULT PORTIONS

vegetable oil
2 onions, peeled and chopped
4 breasts of chicken, on the bone and
skinned
plain flour
salt and pepper
1 red and 1 green sweet pepper,
seeded and cut into strips

1 dessertspoon paprika
2 large tomatoes, skinned, seeded and
cut in small pieces
300 ml/10 fl oz chicken stock
(see page 62)
1 tablespoon cornflour
50 ml/2 fl oz soured cream

In a heavy saucepan heat a little oil and sauté the onion until golden. Meanwhile, roll the chicken in seasoned flour then, in a separate frying pan, brown in a little oil. Drain on kitchen paper. Add the pepper dice, a little salt and paprika to the onion, cook for 3 minutes then add the tomatoes and the chicken stock. Cover and simmer for 5 minutes then add the chicken and cook until tender (about 20 minutes).

Remove the chicken, take it off the bone and cut the flesh into small bite-sized pieces. Mix the cornflour with a little cold water and stir it into the sauce. Bring to the boil, stirring constantly.

Stir the soured cream into the sauce and allow it to simmer (do not let it boil) for a few minutes. Pour over the chicken.

Chicken Fillets with Mango Chutney and Apricot

This is very simple to prepare but tastes absolutely delicious. It is a great favourite with children because of the sweet and sour taste.

MAKES 2 ADULT PORTIONS

2 chicken breasts, off the bone and skinned

Sauce
1 tablespoon apricot jam
1 tablespoon mango chutney
3 tablespoons mayonnaise
1 teaspoon Worcestershire sauce
1 tablespoon lemon juice

Mix all the ingredients together for the sauce. Put the chicken into a small ovenproof dish, pour over the sauce and cover the dish with aluminium foil. Bake in an oven preheated to 350°F(180°C)Gas 4 for 30 minutes.

Stir-Fried Chicken with Vegetables and Noodles

Use the vegetables listed as a guide. As a short-cut, some supermarkets sell packets of ready prepared stir-fry vegetables. The colourful different foods are very appealing to toddlers.

MAKES 6 ADULT PORTIONS

3 breasts of chicken, off the bone and skinned
3 tablespoons soy sauce
1 teaspoon cornflour
2 tablespoons chicken stock
2 teaspoons sugar
100 g/4 oz egg noodles
vegetable oil
1 small onion, peeled

2 baby leeks, trimmed
1 medium carrot, peeled
100 g/4 oz cauliflower
175 g/6 oz cabbage
175 g/6 oz bean sprouts
100 g/4 oz mushrooms
100 g/4 oz mangetout, stringed
6 baby sweetcorn, trimmed
50 g/2 oz sesame seeds, toasted (see page 131)

Cut the chicken into small pieces and marinate it in the soy sauce, cornflour, stock and sugar for at least 2 hours. Drain the marinade from the chicken and reserve. Cook the noodles according to the instructions on the packet then, when cooked, drain and stir in a little oil to prevent them sticking together.

Chop all the vegetables into small pieces. Put 2 tablespoons of oil in a *wok* or frying pan and, when hot, add the chopped onion and leeks. When transparent, add the chicken and cook for about 5 minutes or until the chicken is just cooked through. Add the carrot and cauliflower and cook for 2 minutes with a little of the soy sauce from the marinade. Add the rest of the vegetables and soy sauce and cook for 3–4 minutes depending on how crisp you like them. Add the noodles to the stir-fry, mix thoroughly and sprinkle with the toasted sesame seeds.

Mulligatawny Chicken

This recipe has a tomato base and a mild curry flavour which children love. It has been a family favourite since I was a child and was invented by my mother. It is best served with rice and, for special occasions, you can serve *poppadums* as an accompaniment. They are available in most supermarkets.

MAKES 8 ADULT PORTIONS

1 chicken, cut into about 10 pieces, skinned
plain flour
salt and pepper to taste
vegetable oil
2 medium onions, peeled and chopped
6 tablespoons tomato purée
2 tablespoons mild curry powder
900 ml/1½ pints chicken stock (see page 62)

1 large or 2 small apples, cored and thinly sliced
1 small carrot, peeled and thinly sliced
2 lemon slices
75 g/3 oz sultanas
1 bay leaf
1 dessertspoon brown sugar

Coat the chicken pieces with seasoned flour. Fry in vegetable oil until golden brown. Drain on kitchen paper and place in a casserole dish.

Fry the onion in a little oil until golden, then stir in the tomato purée. Add the curry powder and continue to stir for a couple of minutes over a low heat. Stir in 2 tablespoons of flour, then pour in 300 ml/10 fl oz of the stock, mixing well.

Add the apple, carrot, lemon slices, sultanas, bay leaf and the rest of the stock. Season with brown sugar, salt and pepper. Pour the sauce over the chicken in the casserole, cover and cook for 1 hour in an oven preheated to 350°F(180°C)Gas 4. Remove the lemon slices and bay leaf; take the chicken off the bone and cut it into pieces.

Sesame Chicken Nuggets with Honey Lemon Sauce

These make great finger food. They can be served as a hot meal or they can be eaten cold on their own or cooked in the honey lemon sauce.

MAKES 8 CHICKEN NUGGETS

2 breasts of chicken, off the bone and
skinned
1 egg
1 tablespoon milk
plain flour
sesame seeds
1 tablespoon vegetable oil

Marinade
1 teaspoon soy sauce
¼ teaspoon salt
¼ teaspoon sugar
1 teaspoon cornflour
1 tablespoon water

Sauce
1 tablespoon honey
1 dessertspoon soy sauce
1 teaspoon freshly squeezed lemon
juice

Cut each chicken breast into about four pieces. Combine the ingredients for the marinade and marinate the chicken in this for at least 2 hours.

Beat the egg together with the milk and dip the chicken nuggets into the flour, then into the egg and finally coat with sesame seeds. Fry in hot oil for about 5 minutes, turning the chicken frequently, until golden brown.

Combine the ingredients for the sauce, pour this over the chicken in the frying pan and continue to cook for 2 minutes more.

Sauté of Chicken Livers
with Wheatgerm

MAKES 2 ADULT PORTIONS

2 shallots, peeled and finely chopped
margarine
50 g/2 oz baby carrots, washed and
cut into fine strips
100 g/4 oz chicken livers

1 egg, beaten
2 tablespoons wheatgerm
50 ml/2 fl oz chicken stock
(see page 62)

Fry the shallot in 25 g/1 oz of margarine. After 1 minute, add the carrots and continue to fry for another minute. Dip the prepared liver into the beaten egg then coat with wheatgerm. Fry for about 3 minutes. It may be necessary to add a little more margarine to the frying pan to stop the liver from sticking. Pour over the chicken stock and simmer covered for a further 15 minutes or until the liver is cooked through. Chop the cooked liver into pieces and serve with a little mashed potato.

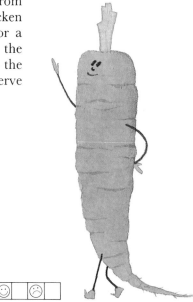

MEAT

Juicy Beefburgers

These are super moist beefburgers. Serve them with chips and
tomato ketchup for a special treat.

MAKES 8 BEEFBURGERS

1 ripe tomato, skinned and seeded
1 medium onion, peeled
1 medium potato, peeled
450 g/1 lb lean minced beef
4 tablespoons wholemeal breadcrumbs
1 tablespoon chopped parsley

1 teaspoon Marmite dissolved in
50 ml/2 fl oz boiling water
black pepper
vegetable oil for frying

Topping
1 onion, peeled, finely sliced and fried
in a little oil

Grate the tomato, onion and potato in a food processor and add to
the meat. Add all the rest of the ingredients and mix well. Heat
some oil in a frying pan and shape the meat into eight patties. Fry for
about 10 minutes, browning the burgers well on each side. Serve with
the fried onion slices on top.

Cocktail Meatballs with Tomato Sauce

This is especially nice served with spaghetti and makes a great meal for the whole family. The meatballs on their own make good finger food and can be eaten either hot or cold.

MAKES 36 SMALL MEATBALLS

450 g/1 lb lean minced beef
1 onion, peeled and finely chopped
1 tablespoon chopped parsley
1 teaspoon Marmite mixed with a little boiling water
1 egg, beaten
salt and pepper
2 thin slices white bread
2 tablespoons milk
plain flour
50 g/2 oz margarine

Tomato sauce
1 onion, peeled and finely chopped
a little margarine
½ red and green sweet pepper, seeded and finely chopped
400 g/14 oz can tomatoes, drained and chopped
2 tablespoons tomato purée
1 teaspoon red wine vinegar
1 tablespoon milk
1 tablespoon chopped basil

In a bowl, mix together the meat, chopped onion, parsley, Marmite, beaten egg and seasoning. Trim the crust off the white bread and soak it in milk for a few minutes, then squeeze out the excess moisture. Break the bread into small pieces and add this to the minced meat. Form the mixture into small balls and roll in seasoned flour. Fry in the margarine until browned all over.

To make the tomato sauce, fry the onion in a little margarine until transparent, then add the sweet pepper and fry for another 4 minutes. Add the tomatoes, tomato purée, vinegar, milk, basil and salt and pepper. Simmer for 10–15 minutes. Put the meatballs into a covered casserole and pour over the tomato sauce. Mix well and cook in an oven preheated to 300°F(150°C)Gas 2 for 1 hour.

Shepherd's Pie

If you have any little ramekin dishes, then it is very nice to make your child his very own little shepherd's pie. Let him see it, and then spoon out of the hot dish on to his plate.

MAKES 6 ADULT PORTIONS

1 onion, peeled and finely chopped
vegetable oil
450 g/1 lb lean minced beef
½ red and green sweet pepper, seeded and finely chopped
1 tablespoon finely chopped parsley
250 ml/8 fl oz chicken stock (see page 62)
1 teaspoon Marmite

salt and pepper
100 g/4 oz button mushrooms, washed and sliced
a little margarine

Topping
450 g/1 lb potatoes, peeled and chopped
15 g/½ oz margarine
50 ml/2 fl oz milk

Fry the chopped onion in a little oil in a saucepan until golden. Meanwhile, in a frying pan, brown the minced meat. When the onions are cooked, add the chopped pepper and parsley and continue to cook for 4–5 minutes. Put meat into a food processor for 30 seconds to make it easier to chew. Add to the pan with the onion mixture and stir in the chicken stock, Marmite and seasonings. Cook over a low heat for about 20 minutes. Meanwhile, sauté the mushrooms in a little oil and add these to the meat when it is cooked.

To make the topping, boil the potatoes in salted water for about 25 minutes. When soft, mash them together with the margarine, milk and some salt and pepper. Spread over the meat either in one large dish or individual ramekins, then cook in the oven preheated to 350°F(180°C)Gas 4 for 10 minutes. Dot the top with margarine and put under a hot grill for about 3 minutes or until brown and crispy.

Benihana Steak

When two years old, my son loved to go to Benihana. Benihana means 'red rose' and is the name given to a chain of Japanese restaurants worldwide which specialise in *Teppan-yaki* cooking. The food is prepared in front of the customers by a Japanese chef who entertains the children by throwing the food and his knives in the air whilst cooking! After lunch the children are entertained upstairs with a Punch and Judy Show.

Needless to say this is something I am not prepared to do in my own kitchen but I have talked to the head chef at Benihana and he has given me some easy-to-prepare Japanese recipes which are great for kids. An optional extra to these recipes is, of course, one silk kimono to be worn by Mum!

MAKES 2 ADULT PORTIONS

150 g/5 oz sirloin steak
2 tablespoons soy sauce
½ teaspoon sugar

2 tablespoons chopped onions
50 g/2 oz button mushrooms, sliced
soya or vegetable oil

Cut the steak into bite-sized cubes. Heat the soy sauce with the sugar until the sugar has dissolved. Marinate the steak in the soy sauce, sugar and chopped onion for about 30 minutes.

Drain off the soy sauce and onions and set aside. Heat the oil in a frying pan and when it is hot, fry the meat until tender. Remove the meat and fry the onion and mushrooms. Combine the steak, mushrooms and onion and serve.

Veal Stroganoff

Veal is easier than beef for your toddler to chew. This recipe is quick and easy to make and delicious. It is very nice as a family meal served with noodles and, to give it an authentic stroganoff taste, you can even add a dollop of soured cream.

MAKES 2 ADULT PORTIONS

cooking oil
1 onion, peeled and very finely chopped
½ red and yellow sweet pepper, seeded and cut into strips
225 g/8 oz thin veal escalope, cut into strips

plain flour
salt and pepper
300 ml/10 fl oz chicken stock (see page 62)
175 g/6 oz button mushrooms, washed and sliced

Heat a little oil in a frying pan and sauté the onion for 3–4 minutes. Add the strips of sweet pepper and continue to cook for 1 more minute. Roll the strips of veal in seasoned flour and cook these in the frying pan for about 3 minutes or until browned (add a little more oil if you find the veal is sticking to the pan).

Pour the chicken stock over the veal and stir in the mushrooms and some salt and pepper. Simmer, covered, for about 8 minutes.

Celery Chops

MAKES 4 ADULT PORTIONS

4 lamb chops	a little black pepper
vegetable oil	1/2 celery stalk, finely chopped
2 tablespoons brown sugar	1/2 small onion, finely chopped
a few drops Worcestershire sauce	1/2 green pepper, finely chopped
1 tablespoon lemon juice	4 tablespoons tomato ketchup

Brown the chops in a little oil and sauté the celery and onion for 4 minutes. Mix together the brown sugar, Worcestershire sauce, lemon juice and black pepper. Brush over the chops. Sprinkle the celery onion and pepper over the chops and pour over the tomato ketchup. Bake at 325°F(160°C)Gas 3 for 1 hour.

Liver and Onion

You are doing a great job if your children enjoy liver.

MAKES 1–2 ADULT PORTIONS

1/2 onion, peeled and chopped	2 tablespoons chopped mushrooms
1 tablespoon finely chopped green pepper	1 medium tomato, skinned, seeded and chopped
vegetable oil	100 g/4 oz calf's liver

Fry the chopped onion and pepper in a little oil until the onions are very brown. Add the chopped mushrooms and tomato and fry for another 2 minutes. Fry the liver for 1 1/2 minutes each side. When the liver is cooked cut into small pieces and cover with the vegetables.

PASTA

Spinach Pasta Sauce

This is a delicious sauce which is good with any type of pasta.

MAKES 2 ADULT PORTIONS

225 g/8 oz fresh, washed spinach,
tough stalks removed (or use frozen)
25 g/1 oz margarine
15 g/¹/₂ oz plain flour

250 ml/8 fl oz milk
2 tablespoons grated Parmesan cheese
a pinch of freshly grated nutmeg
salt and pepper to taste

Cook the spinach in very little water for about 5 minutes, then drain, reserving 2 tablespoons of the cooking liquid.

Meanwhile make a white sauce with the margarine, flour and milk (see page 59). Bring to the boil, then simmer for 2–3 minutes. Add the reserved spinach liquid, together with the Parmesan and nutmeg.

Finely chop the spinach in a food processor and stir this into the sauce. Season with salt and pepper. Serve with the cooked pasta of your choice and sprinkle with a little extra Parmesan cheese.

Penne with Courgettes and Cheese

Children love pasta which they can pick up with their fingers.

MAKES 4 ADULT PORTIONS

450 g/1 lb courgettes, sliced
70 ml/2½ fl oz olive oil
225 g/8 oz penne (tubes)

100 g/4 oz Mozzarella cheese, cubed
1 egg, beaten
25 g/1 oz grated Parmesan cheese

Fry the courgette slices lightly in olive oil. Take care not to over-cook them as they should be just tender. Cook the pasta according to instructions on the packet but make sure that it is *al dente*.

Heat a serving bowl and as soon as the pasta is cooked, drain it and pour it into the bowl. Add the cubed Mozzarella and stir well until all the cheese has melted. Add the beaten egg and courgettes, stirring quickly, then sprinkle with the Parmesan cheese. Brown under hot grill, then serve immediately.

Macaroni Cheese with Ketchup

This tasty macaroni cheese has a lovely crunchy topping.

MAKES 3 ADULT PORTIONS

100 g/4 oz macaroni
salt
15 g/½ oz margarine
1 tablespoon plain flour
175 ml/6 fl oz milk
25 g/1 oz Cheddar cheese, grated
1 tablespoon tomato ketchup

1 dessertspoon snipped chives
(optional)

Topping
2 tablespoons wholemeal breadcrumbs
25 g/1 oz Cheddar cheese, grated
a little margarine

Cook the macaroni in boiling salted water according to the instructions on the packet. Use the margarine, flour and milk to make a thick white sauce (see page 59). Remove from the heat and stir in the cheese, tomato ketchup and chives, if using.

Put the macaroni into an ovenproof dish and mix with the sauce. Sprinkle with the breadcrumbs and grated cheese and dot with margarine. Brown under the grill for 2–3 minutes to make a crispy topping.

Spaghetti Primavera

Spaghetti with vegetables makes a delicious and colourful dish. Be careful not to overcook the vegetables or they will be soft and mushy.

MAKES 4 ADULT PORTIONS

25 g/1 oz margarine
4 tomatoes, skinned, seeded and chopped
1 tablespoon chopped basil
100 g/4 oz mushrooms, washed and sliced
50 ml/2 fl oz milk

100 g/4 oz each of small cauliflower and broccoli florets
2 courgettes, trimmed and cut into 5 mm/¼ inch slices
100 g/4 oz spaghettini or tagliolini
freshly grated Parmesan cheese

Melt the margarine in a small frying pan and fry the tomato and basil for 2 minutes. Add the mushrooms and cook for a further 3 minutes. Stir in the milk and continue to cook for 2 minutes.

Meanwhile, steam the remaining vegetables until they are just tender and cook the pasta according to the instructions on the packet.

Add the steamed vegetables to the mushrooms and tomatoes. Cook over a gentle heat for 2 minutes then add to the cooked pasta and mix well. Sprinkle with Parmesan and serve immediately.

Chicken Liver in Tomato Sauce with Pasta

This is a good recipe to encourage your child to eat liver. In fact, I have found that some young children who normally dislike liver will eat it when it is mixed up with pasta. Any pasta can be used but it is particularly appealing to young children with fusilli in three colours, which can be bought at most supermarkets.

MAKES 3 ADULT PORTIONS

½ small onion, peeled and finely chopped
vegetable oil
½ small red sweet pepper, seeded and chopped
50 g/2 oz mushrooms, washed and sliced

1 or 2 chicken livers, cleaned and sliced
2 tablespoons tomato purée
120 ml/4 fl oz chicken stock (see page 62)
1 dessertspoon chopped parsley
75 g/3 oz pasta

Gently sauté the onion in a little oil. When it is soft and transparent, add the red pepper and mushrooms. Continue to cook for 2–3 minutes and then add the liver slices together with the tomato purée, chicken stock and chopped parsley. Cover and simmer gently for about 10 minutes or until the liver is tender. Cook the pasta according to packet instructions, drain, then pour the sauce over.

Animal Pasta Salad with Multi-Coloured Vegetables

I make this recipe with multi-coloured animal-shaped pasta. Toddlers love picking out all the different ingredients. It looks very attractive and colourful on a plate and can be served warm or cold. You can omit the chicken for a vegetarian dish.

MAKES 4 ADULT PORTIONS

100 g/4 oz multi-coloured pasta shapes
1 chicken breast, skinned and cut into bite-sized pieces
vegetable oil
3 baby carrots, or 1 medium carrot, cut into fine strips
100 g/4 oz button mushrooms, washed and sliced
50 g/2 oz each of cauliflower and broccoli, cut into small florets
3 courgettes, trimmed and sliced

50 g/2 oz French beans, chopped
100 g/4 oz frozen sweetcorn
½ sweet red pepper, finely chopped
sugar

Dressing
2 tablespoons cider or red wine vinegar
salt and black pepper
50 ml/2 fl oz olive oil
2 spring onions, finely sliced, or 2 tablespoons snipped chives

Cook the pasta according to the packet instructions, drain. Fry the chicken in a little oil for 2 minutes, then add the carrots and mushrooms and continue to cook for a further 5 minutes. Meanwhile steam the cauliflower, broccoli, courgettes and beans until cooked but still crisp. The cauliflower and broccoli will need a little longer than the courgettes and beans. Cook the sweetcorn and red pepper in water with a little salt and sugar for 5 minutes.

To prepare the dressing, whisk the vinegar with salt and pepper, then whisk in the olive oil a little at a time. Add the spring onions. Combine all the ingredients together and pour the dressing over.

FRUIT AND DESSERTS

Banana Split

This is simple to make and very healthy to eat. It looks attractive laid out on a plate, especially if you include some more exotic fruits like kiwi and mango.

MAKES 1 ADULT PORTION

1 banana
1 tablespoon cottage cheese

3 tablespoons of a variety of fruits, cut into small cubes

Peel the banana and split it in half lengthwise. Lay the two halves side by side on a plate with the two ends touching one another. Spread the cottage cheese in the centre of the bananas and pile the chopped fruit on top.

Peach Melba Delight

A healthy alternative to this favourite ice-cream dessert.

MAKES 2 ADULT PORTIONS

150 g/5 oz Greek yoghurt
1 small 60 g/2¼ oz carton fromage frais
1 teaspoon caster sugar (optional)

1 peach, skinned and cut into small pieces
175 g/6 oz raspberries
1 tablespoon cornflakes, crushed

Mix the yoghurt, fromage frais and sugar. Stir in the fruit and sprinkle with crushed cornflakes.

Snow-Covered Fruit Salad

Try this combination of fruits which are all rich in Vitamin C, better than any vitamin tablets. You can make your own combination according to what is in season.

MAKES 5 ADULT PORTIONS

1 peach, skinned, stoned and cut into small pieces

1 papaya, peeled, seeded and cut into small chunks

8 strawberries, washed, hulled and cut into quarters

2 oranges, peeled, pith removed and cut into chunks

1 tablespoon rasperries or blackberries

½ small canteloupe melon, flesh removed and cut into chunks

100 g/4 oz cherries, stoned and halved

1 small wedge of watermelon, flesh removed and cut into chunks

2 kiwi fruit, peeled and sliced juice of 1 orange

Topping
450 g/1 lb natural yoghurt
2 tablespoons honey
2 tablespoons wheatgerm or muesli

Combine all the fruits together in a large bowl. Pour the orange juice over them and mix well.

Mix the yoghurt with the honey and wheatgerm or muesli and pour over the fruit just before serving.

Peaches with Amaretto Biscuits

Amaretto biscuits are small round macaroons from Italy which are wrapped in pairs in tissue paper. If you cannot find them, you could substitute crushed macaroon biscuits. This is very simple to make, looks very attractive and tastes delicious! (If you are making it for adults, then try substituting Amaretto liqueur for the apple juice.)

MAKES 4 ADULT PORTIONS

2 ripe peaches
4 Amaretto biscuits

85 ml/3 fl oz apple juice
⅛ teaspoon almond essence

Wash the peaches and cut them in half. Carefully remove the stones. Lay the peaches skin side down in an ovenproof dish. Place an Amaretto biscuit in the hollow of each peach. Mix together the apple juice and almond essence and pour this over the peaches. Cover the dish with aluminium foil and bake in the oven preheated to 350°F(180°C)Gas 4 for 15–20 minutes. The peaches can be eaten hot or cold.

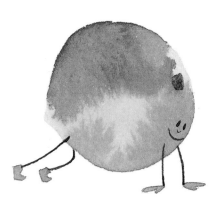

Apple Crumble

I like a lot of fruit in my crumble so this recipe tends to have a larger proportion of fruit than crumble. By using naturally sweet eating apples instead of cooking apples, you do not need to cook the apples first and you do not need to add sugar to the fruit.

As an alternative, substitute 350 g/12 oz rhubarb, 75 g/3 oz brown sugar and the juice of a small orange for the apples and cinnamon to make rhubarb crumble. Or use the apple and blackberry mixture on page 86.

MAKES 6 ADULT PORTIONS

*6 eating apples, peeled, cored and
thinly sliced
¹/₂ teaspoon powdered cinnamon
2 tablespoons water*

Crumble topping
*100 g/4 oz plain flour or
¹/₂ plain and ¹/₂ wholemeal
75 g/3 oz margarine or butter, cut
into pieces
50 g/2 oz caster sugar
50 g/2 oz rolled oats
a pinch of salt*

For the crumble topping, sift the flour into a mixing bowl, add the margarine or butter pieces and rub in. Add the sugar, oats and salt and continue rubbing until the mixture clings together in large crumbs.

Put the apple slices into a fairly deep round dish and add the cinnamon and water. Top with the crumble mixture and bake in the oven preheated to 350°F(180°C)Gas 4 for 30 minutes, by which time the top of the crumble should have turned a golden brown.

Easy No-Bake Cheesecake

This is one of the most delicious cheesecakes I have tasted, and the recipe was given to me by a friend, Maureen Kerzner. It is very smooth and creamy and takes no more than 15 minutes to make. If you want to serve it to adults and impress your friends, soak the biscuits in a mixture of milk and brandy instead of apple juice.

MAKES 15 ADULT PORTIONS

Base
40 sponge finger biscuits soaked in
175 ml/6 fl oz apple juice

Topping
125 g/4½ oz packet lemon jelly
175 ml/6 fl oz boiling water
250 g/9 oz evaporated milk
675 g/1½ lb low-fat cream cheese
90 g/3½ oz caster sugar
1 teaspoon vanilla essence
250 ml/8 fl oz whipping cream
powdered cinnamon

Dissolve the jelly in the boiling water. In a large bowl, mix together the evaporated milk, cream cheese, sugar and vanilla. Stir in the cooled jelly mixture. Beat the whipping cream until it stands up in soft peaks. Fold the cream into the jelly mixture.

Lay half the softened biscuits in the base of a tin 25 cm/10 inches x 7.5 cm/3 inches. Pour half the cheese mixture over the biscuit base, top with a layer of the remaining soaked biscuits. Pour over the remaining cheese mixture and allow to set in the fridge for several hours. Dust the top with cinnamon.

Cherry Pie

Make this simple delicious dessert when cherries are in season.

MAKES 6 ADULT PORTIONS

75 g/3 oz plain flour, sifted
50 g/2 oz caster sugar
a pinch of salt
3 eggs

450 ml/15 fl oz milk
450 g/1 lb cherries, stoned
25 g/1 oz margarine or butter
caster sugar for sprinkling on top

Make a well in the flour and blend in the sugar, salt and eggs. Beat in the milk gradually to a smooth batter. Spread the cherries in a greased ovenproof dish and pour over the batter. Dot margarine on top and bake at 350°F (180°C) Gas 4 for 35–40 minutes. Sprinkle with sugar.

Grandma's Lokshen Pudding

Lokshen is vermicelli, very fine egg noodles. This easy dessert is one of my all-time favourites. For variation, add a few flaked almonds.

MAKES 8 ADULT PORTIONS

225 g/8 oz vermicelli
175 g/6 oz each of sultanas, currants
or raisins
1 large egg, beaten

50g/2 oz margarine, melted
1 dessertspoon brown sugar
³/₄ teaspoon cinnamon or mixed spice

Cook the vermicelli in boiling water for about 5 minutes. Mix the remaining ingredients together and then mix with the drained vermicelli. Placed in a greased shallow baking dish, dot with extra margarine and bake for 30 minutes at 300°F (150°C) Gas 2.

Home-made Dairy Ice Cream

Home-made ice cream is always delicious but often contains eggs, sugar and lots of double cream. Whipping cream has a much lower fat content than double cream or you could use Greek or natural yoghurt. You may want to add a little honey or sugar to sweeten the ice cream if using all or some yoghurt instead of cream. Add different flavourings or fruit purées to this basic dairy ice cream for a host of delicious yet healthy frozen desserts.

MAKES 6 ADULT PORTIONS

215 g/7½ oz skimmed evaporated milk
2 teaspoons powdered gelatine

150 ml/5 fl oz whipping cream or 225 g/8 oz Greek or natural yoghurt or ½ quantity of yoghurt and ½ of cream

Chill the evaporated milk and then whisk until very thick and foamy. Dissolve the gelatine by sprinkling over 3 tablespoons of very hot water. Add the gelatine to the whisked evaporated milk, folding it in gently. Chill for 30 minutes. Whip the cream to soft peaks and fold into the whisked mixture and/or fold in the yoghurt. Spoon into a freezerproof container. Freeze for 2 hours, then remove from the freezer and whisk thoroughly. Return to the freezer until firm. Soften at room temperature for 15 minutes before serving.

For variations add fruit purées or other flavours after the cream.
Peach and Redcurrant. 120 ml/4 fl oz peach purée and 2 tablespoons of redcurrant jelly.
Pear and Ginger. 175 ml/6 fl oz pear purée and ¼ teaspoon ginger.
Berry Fruit. 175 ml/6 fl oz any berry fruit purée such as strawberry, raspberry, blackberry, loganberry or a mixture. Sieve before using.
Exotic Fruit. 175 ml/6 fl oz mango, papaya, lychee, pineapple, cantaloupe purée or a combination of any of these.
Halva. 100 g/4 oz flaked halva.
Maple Choc Chip. 2 tablespoons maple syrup and 3 tablespoons chocolate chips.

Iced Lollies

Iced lollies are always popular with children. You can buy lolly moulds with re-usable plastic sticks. Fill the moulds with your chosen fruit purée or fruit juice, put the plastic sticks on top (these also serve as covers) and freeze on a level surface in the freezer. Dip the mould into warm water when you want to get an iced lolly out. Or use plastic or paper cups, cover with foil, pierce with a wooden stick and let it almost touch the bottom of the cup.

You can make your own fruit purées from fresh fruits in season or you can use natural fruit juices as the basis of your lollies. Sweeten to taste with sugar or honey and stir Greek or natural yoghurt into fresh fruit purée for a frozen yoghurt lolly. These pure ingredients are much better for your child than commercial iced lollies many of which are full of additives, colourings and sugar.

My son Nicholas, when two years old, had fairly sophisticated taste and developed a penchant for passion-fruit ice lollies (as did his father, who goes straight for the freezer after supper!). Try also blackcurrant (Ribena) pineapple juice, concentrated orange juice and sparkling apple juice.

Two-tone iced lollies are fun. Half-fill the moulds with purée of one colour, freeze then pour over a purée of a contrasting colour.

Fruit Salad Lollies

MAKES 6 ICED LOLLIES

1 apple, peeled and cored
1 pear, peeled and cored
1 orange, peeled and segmented

1 small banana
120 ml/4 fl oz freshly squeezed
orange juice

Combine in a blender or processor and blend until smooth. Pour into moulds and freeze. ☺ ☹

BAKING FOR TODDLERS

Traditional English Fruit Cake

This is a dark rich fruit cake which is great served in small pieces for a tea-time treat. The cake can keep very well for one month (that is, if Mummy and Daddy haven't got to it first). If you are making this cake for adults, it tastes wonderful if you soak the fruit in a mixture of brandy and port instead of orange juice.

MAKES 16 ADULT PORTIONS

275 g/10 oz each currants and sultanas	*150 g/5 oz mixed peel*
350 g/12 oz raisins	*100 g/4 oz glacé cherries, chopped*
175 ml/6 fl oz orange juice	*225 g/8 oz plain flour*
225 g/8 oz margarine or butter	*1 teaspoon baking soda*
150 g/5 oz brown sugar	*¹/₂ teaspoon salt*
4 eggs	*2 teaspoons powdered cinnamon*
100 g/4 oz chopped walnuts	*1 teaspoon ground ginger*
	2 teaspoons mixed spice

Sprinkle the dried fruit with the orange juice and leave for about 2 hours. Cream the margarine together with the sugar then beat in the eggs one at a time. Add the fruits and their liquid, the walnuts, peel and cherries.

Mix together all the remaining dry ingredients and fold these into the batter.

Line the bottom of a 25 cm/10 in round cake tin with greased greaseproof paper and pour in the cake mix. Bake in a slow oven preheated to 300–325°F (150–160°C) Gas 2–3 for 2 to 2¹/₂ hours. Leave to get cold, then store in an airtight container.

Tea-Time Apple Treat

This is a lovely moist cake with lots of apple slices on top. Cut this cake into squares and watch them vanish at your child's tea party.

MAKES 12 SQUARES

65 g/2¹/₂ oz brown sugar
165 g/5¹/₂ oz plain flour
¹/₂ teaspoon baking powder
¹/₂ teaspoon baking soda
a pinch of salt
1 egg
50 ml/2 fl oz vegetable oil
120 ml/4 fl oz apple purée (see page 24)
50 g/2 oz apple or vanilla yoghurt
¹/₂ teaspoon vanilla essence

Topping
3 eating apples peeled, cored and finely sliced
1 teaspoon powdered cinnamon

Glaze
4 tablespoons apricot jam
1 tablespoon water
1 tablespoon lemon juice

Mix all the dry ingredients together in a bowl. Beat the egg with the oil, apple purée, yoghurt and vanilla. Add the apple purée mixture to the dry ingredients and stir until blended.

Pour the batter into a greased shallow rectangular cake tin, 25 x 15 cm (10 x 6 in) and arrange the apple slices in lines over it. Sprinkle the cinnamon over the apples and bake in an oven preheated to 350°F(180°C)Gas 4 for 35 minutes.

For the glaze, put all the ingredients in a small pan and cook over a low heat for 1 minute. Sieve and brush the glaze over the apple slices.

Smartie Fairy Cakes

These little cakes can be frozen, best done before they are iced.
They are ideal for a birthday celebration, but you might find the
children are more interested in picking off the sweets than they are
in eating the cakes!

MAKES 18 CAKES

100 g/4 oz soft unsalted butter
150 g/5 oz sugar
2 eggs
1/2 teaspoon vanilla essence
200 g/7 oz sponge flour
2 teaspoons baking powder
1/4 teaspoon salt
70 ml/2 1/2 fl oz milk
170 g/6 oz raisins (optional)
1 packet candy-coated chocolate beans

Chocolate icing
25 g/1 oz chocolate
25 g/1 oz soft unsalted butter
100g/4 oz icing sugar, sifted
1 teaspoon milk

Cream cheese icing
50 g/2 oz unsalted butter
225 g/8 oz icing sugar
1 teaspoon vanilla essence
100 g/4 oz cream cheese

Cream butter and sugar together until light and fluffy, then beat in
the eggs one at a time. Add the vanilla. Sift the dry ingredients
together and add to the mixture, a little at a time, alternating with the
milk. If you are using raisins, add them to the batter. Half fill little
paper cups set into cup-cake baking trays and bake in an oven preheated to 400°F(200°C)Gas 6 for 15 minutes.

I like to make two different coloured icings, so I use chocolate and
then a pale cream cheese icing. If you prefer, make a simple glacé
icing; divide into two before you add the colouring, and then use
different colours for each half.

For the chocolate icing, melt the chocolate in a double boiler. Beat
the butter with a fork until soft, then stir in the sugar a little at a time,
adding a little milk to make the icing thinner. Stir in the melted
chocolate, mix thoroughly and spread the icing over some of the
cakes. (If too thick to spread, add a little more milk.) Put a few candy-

coated chocolate beans on top of the icing for decoration.

For the cream cheese icing, beat the butter, sugar and vanilla until crumbly. Stir in the cream cheese. Do not over beat or it will become watery. Spread over the cakes and decorate with candy-coated chocolate beans.

☺ ☹

Bran Muffins with Apples and Raisins

These are absolutely delicious and very healthy too; they never last long in our house!

MAKES ABOUT 15 MUFFINS

120 ml/4 fl oz vegetable oil
2 tablespoons honey
2 tablespoons maple syrup
175 ml/6 fl oz milk
175 ml/6 fl oz apple juice
2 eggs, beaten

225 g/8 oz self-raising flour
100 g/4 oz bran
2 tablespoons baking powder
1/2 teaspoon salt
2 apples, peeled and grated
175 g/6 oz raisins

Mix together the oil, honey and maple syrup. Add the milk, apple juice and beaten eggs. In another bowl mix the flour, bran, baking powder and salt together. Combine the liquid ingredients with the dry ingredients then fold in the grated apple and raisins. Spoon the batter into a muffin tray or a baking tray for individual small cakes lined with paper cup cases and bake in the oven preheated to 350°F(180°C)Gas 4 for 30 minutes.

☺ ☹

Yoghurt Magimix Cake

This cake has a lovely flavour and a very moist texture. It takes no more than 5 minutes to prepare. If you wish, you can make it in two round cake tins instead of one, and sandwich them together with the cream cheese icing from page 174.

MAKES 8 ADULT PORTIONS

160 g/5¼ oz sugar
250 ml/8 fl oz vegetable oil
225 g/8 oz natural set yoghurt
2 eggs

225 g/8 oz extra light sponge flour
3 teaspoons baking powder
2 teaspoons vanilla essence
icing sugar

Grease a 25 cm/10 in round chiffon cake tin. In a blender or food processor, mix the sugar with the oil, then add the yoghurt and mix. Blend with the eggs, flour, baking powder and vanilla. Pour into the prepared tin and bake at 325–350°F(160–180°C)Gas 3–4 for 55 minutes. Sprinkle the top with sugar when cold.

White Chocolate Button Cookies

These are so easy to make and are really delicious. Baked for only 12 minutes, they should be quite soft when they are taken out of the oven so that when they cool down they are lovely and moist.

MAKES 20 COOKIES

100 g/4 oz unsalted butter or
margarine at room temperature
100 g/4 oz caster sugar
100 g/4 oz brown sugar
1 egg
1 teaspoon vanilla essence

175 g/6 oz plain flour
½ teaspoon baking powder
¼ teaspoon salt
175 g/6 oz white chocolate buttons
75 g/3 oz pecans or walnuts, chopped
(optional)

Beat the butter together with the sugars. With a fork, beat the egg together with the vanilla and add this to the butter mixture.

In a bowl, mix together the flour, baking powder and salt. Add this to the butter and egg mixture and blend well.

Break the chocolate buttons into smaller pieces with a rolling pin or in a food processor, and stir these together with the nuts (if used) into the mixture.

Line several baking sheets with non-stick baking paper and roll the dough into walnut-sized balls. Put these on to the sheets, spaced well apart, and bake in an oven preheated to 375°F(190°C)Gas 5 for 12 minutes. Take carefully off the baking paper and let them cool.

Chewy Muesli Squares

Give these to your child as a healthy treat.

MAKES 20 SMALL SQUARES

100 g/4 oz margarine or butter
1 tablespoon honey
1 tablespoon malt extract
1/2 teaspoon vanilla essence
1/2 teaspoon bicarbonate of soda
65 g/2 1/2 oz unsweetened muesli

25 g/1 oz oats
40 g/1 1/2 oz desiccated coconut
40 g/1 1/2 oz sesame seeds
40 g/1 1/2 oz sultanas
1 tablespoon demerara sugar

Melt the margarine together with the honey and malt extract in a saucepan, then add the vanilla and bicarbonate of soda. Mix all the remaining ingredients in a bowl, pour in the melted mixture, and stir well.

Put the mixture into a baking tin, 18 cm/7 inches square and bake in the oven preheated to 350°F(180°C)Gas 4 for 30 minutes.

Funny Shape Biscuits

Biscuit cutters come in all sorts of weird and wonderful shapes. I use a gingerbread cutter and animal cutouts and my son can't wait to get his hands on the biscuits. I get a running commentary as to which piece of the anatomy he has just eaten!

MAKES 15–20 BISCUITS depending on size of cutters

50 g/2 oz wholemeal flour
100 g/4 oz plain white flour
75 g/3 oz semolina
¼ teaspoon each ground ginger,
cinnamon, salt

75 g/3 oz margarine or butter
1 medium ripe banana
1½ tablespoons maple syrup
cream cheese for spreading
a few raisins

Put the flours, semolina, ginger, cinnamon and salt into a mixing bowl and rub in the margarine. Mash the banana well with the maple syrup and stir into the mixture to make a smooth pliable dough.

Roll out on lightly floured surface and cut into shapes with biscuit cutters. Bake on lightly greased baking trays in an oven preheated to 400°F(200°C)Gas 6 for 20 minutes until golden and firm. Cool on a wire rack.

If you wish, spread the cooled biscuits with cream cheese, marking with a fork to represent the various animal's fur. Use pieces of raisin for eyes and noses. ☺ ☹

Cheese Pretzels

These are delicious and great fun to make. Your children will enjoy helping you twist the pretzels into different shapes. You can even make letters of the alphabet and spell your child's name!

MAKES 20–30 PRETZELS

1 packet dried yeast
300 ml/10 fl oz warm water
450 g/1 lb plain flour

175 g/6 oz Cheddar cheese, grated
1 egg, beaten
sesame seeds

Dissolve the yeast in the warm water. Stir in the flour and grated cheese. Knead the dough with your hands on a floured board. Break off small pieces of dough and roll into long strands of about 30 cm/12 inches in length and twist into shapes. Put the pretzels on a baking tray lined with non-stick baking paper, brush with beaten egg and sprinkle with sesame seeds. Bake for 20 minutes in the oven preheated to 475°F(250°C)Gas 9.

HEALTHY SNACKS

Fruit Snacks

Wash fruit well. Peel, core, seed or stone and trim as needed.

Bananas, whole or cut into pieces

Chunks of peeled and cored apples

Chunks of pear

Orange, mandarin or clementine segments with as much of the pith removed as possible (make sure there are no pips in the fruit)

Kiwi fruit, peeled and sliced

Strawberries, hulled and halved

Seedless grapes, skinned for babies under one year

Melon, peeled and cut into bite-sized pieces

Peaches, skinned and sliced

Mango, peeled and sliced

Papaya, peeled, seeds removed and cut in thick slices

Raspberries, washed carefully

Lychees, peeled and stoned (toddlers can easily choke on lychee stones)

Pineapple, peeled and cut into chunks

Dried fruit (apricots, prunes, raisins etc). If too tough soak in boiling water

Chocolate-Dipped Fruit

A very appealing way of giving fruit to children is to melt some dark chocolate in a double boiler, dip the tip of the fruit piece into the chocolate and pierce the fruit with a cocktail stick. Stick the cocktail sticks with the fruit into an orange and put this into the fridge to allow the chocolate to harden. Strawberries, pineapple chunks and orange or tangerine segments are especially nice. Remember to remove the cocktail sticks before giving the fruit to your child.

Whole bananas can be coated in chocolate. Place on waxed paper and freeze or chill until the chocolate has set.

If you are worried about your child having too much chocolate, use carob as a substitute.

Vegetable Snacks

As with fruit, wash, peel, trim, and seed as appropriate.

Toddlers love to dip raw vegetables into a sauce and a nicely arranged selection of crudités is great for a toddler who is teething. Try some of the simple but delicious dip recipes that follow. Think also about things like *hummous* – made from chickpeas and which can be bought in most supermarkets – or curd cheese mixed with a little tomato purée which makes a nice creamy dip.

Carrots and cabbage, grated or chopped, mixed with a little mayonnaise and raisins, makes a simple and nutritious snack piled on to lettuce leaves.

Cheese Snacks

Cheese makes an ideal snack for toddlers. Try using a cookie cutter to make animal shapes from slices of cheese. Edam, Gruyère and Emmenthal are particular favourites with most children. Individual cheeses like the small round Babybel and the wrapped triangles of cheese are ideal as well.

Cottage cheese is also popular, plain or simply mixed with something like chopped pineapple. You could also make a scoopful of cheese into a ball, accompany it with a scoopful of grated apple mixed with raisins, and surround it with a selection of mixed fruit chopped very small. This makes a nutritious, yet delicious snack.

Cottage Cheese Dip

MAKES 4 ADULT PORTIONS

125 g/4¹/₂ oz carton cottage cheese
2 tablespoons cream cheese
Worcestershire sauce to taste

1 dessertspoon chopped spring onions
or chives
salt and pepper to taste

Mix all the ingredients together. Serve with a selection of vegetables cut into sticks or strips of pitta bread to dip in.

Green Goddess Dip

MAKES 10 ADULT PORTIONS

1 avocado
¼ cucumber, diced
6 cherry tomatoes, or 2 small
tomatoes, chopped very small
½ small red pepper, seeded and diced
(optional)

¼ small onion, peeled and finely
chopped
2 tablespoons Greek yoghurt
a squeeze of lemon juice
salt and pepper to taste

Cut the avocado in half, stone and scoop the flesh out of the skin. Mash it together with the rest of the ingredients.

Rice Crispie Cheese Balls

Your toddler will enjoy helping to shape the dough into balls.

MAKES 12 BALLS

75 g/3 oz plain flour
50 g/2 oz margarine
½ teaspoon mustard powder
25 g/1 oz Cheddar cheese, grated

50 g/2 oz Parmesan cheese, grated
40 g/1½ oz Rice Crispies
1 egg, beaten
50 g/2 oz sesame seeds

Cream together the flour, margarine, mustard and cheeses. Add the rice crispies and shape the dough with your hands into small balls. Dip the balls into beaten egg, roll in sesame seeds and bake for 20 minutes in an oven preheated to 350°F(180°C)Gas 4.

Home-Made Fast-Food Pizza

A delicious, easy-to-make pizza, a tea-time treat. The Bel Paese cheese gives it a wonderful flavour but you can substitute Mozzarella.

MAKES 2 ADULT PORTIONS

1 spring onion, finely sliced
2 tomatoes, skinned, seeded and chopped
4 button mushrooms, washed and sliced

margarine
1 dessertspoon tomato purée
1 dessertspoon chopped basil
¼ French stick
40 g/1½ oz Bel Paese cheese, sliced

Sauté the spring onion, tomatoes and mushrooms in a little margarine for 2–3 minutes then stir in the tomato purée and basil. Cut the bread in half and spread a little margarine on both halves. Spread the tomato mixture over the bread and put the cheese slices on top. Cook under a hot grill for 3–4 minutes until golden and bubbling.

Stuffed Eggs

Cut hard-boiled eggs in half lengthwise and cut a thin sliver off the base of each half so that they stand firm. Fill with finely mashed yolks mixed with one of the following. Remember that the hollow of a boiled egg is quite small, so you do not need a lot of filling.

chopped cucumber, lettuce, tomato, and mayonnaise

OR

cottage cheese and chives

OR

poached salmon and mayonnaise

finely chopped chicken and tomato ketchup

OR

canned salmon or tuna, mayonnaise and chopped spring onion

Top Hat Egg

This is a great snack to give children for a special tea party.

MAKES 1 ADULT PORTION

1 thick slice of bread
a little butter or margarine
1 egg

1 slice of tomato
25 g/1 oz Cheddar cheese, grated

With a small glass or egg cup, press out a small round from the centre of the bread. Fry the holed slice of bread in some butter for a few seconds on each side, then break the egg carefully into the hole in the bread. When the egg is almost cooked, place the slice of tomato on top and turn the bread back over carefully. Fry the tomato for a few seconds at the same time as the cut-out round of bread. Put the slice of bread under a hot grill with the circle of bread on top of the tomato, and sprinkle with cheese. Grill until golden brown.

French Toast with Marmite

This makes excellent finger food and can be served with boiled or scrambled egg to make a complete meal.

MAKES 1 ADULT PORTION

1 slice of wholemeal bread
½ teaspoon Marmite

1 egg
a little butter or margarine

Thinly spread the Marmite on both sides of the bread. Beat the egg and pour it on to a flat plate. Soak the bread in the egg. Meanwhile melt a little butter in a frying pan, then fry the bread until golden on both sides. Cut the bread into 'soldiers', removing the crusts if your child prefers.

Sandwiches

Sandwiches can come in all shapes and sizes. Try making animal-shaped sandwiches using a cookie cutter. Pinwheel sandwiches are very appealing too (see page 186). Toasted sandwiches are a meal in themselves and it is well worth investing in a toasted sandwich maker which seals the bread.

Try using lots of different breads: small round pitta bread, slit and stuffed with salad; raisin bread; open sandwiches on bridge rolls; bagels (excellent for a toddler to chew on when he is teething); French bread; pumpernickel bread (which is black); or even a sandwich where one side is white and one side is brown.

Presentation is very important. A child is more likely to eat something that looks appealing. Sprinkle the sandwiches with salad cress or decorate with thinly serrated vegetables or make your sandwiches into little trains or boats. It doesn't take long and it's fun to do. I think you will find that a lot of toddlers will reach out for your sandwiches.

On the following pages are some suggestions for sandwich fillings. Your toddler will soon let you know his preferences!

Pinwheel Sandwiches

Ideally the bread for pinwheel sandwiches should be very thin. You can either thinly slice the bread yourself, or you can flatten slices with a rolling pin. If you don't flatten the bread first, it will not be pliable enough to roll without breaking. Cut off all the crusts, and spread the bread evenly with softened butter or margarine and the desired filling (which should be fairly smooth and creamy). Roll up slices with the filling on the inside and cut into slices to make little pinwheels.

You can even make a variegated pinwheel sandwich by rolling one brown and one white slice of bread (which have both been spread with different but complementary fillings) together.

Peanut butter and raspberry jam
Peanut butter and mashed banana
Peanut butter and apple purée
Peanut butter, grated apple and toasted sesame seeds (or chopped raisins)
Cream cheese, Marmite and shredded lettuce

Cream or curd cheese, toasted sesame seeds and mustard and cress

Cream cheese and crushed pine-apple (or fruit purée)

Cream cheese and cucumber

Cream cheese and crushed corn-flakes

Cream cheese in raisin bread with strawberry jam

Cream cheese in a bagel with slices of smoked salmon

Cream cheese with chopped dried apricots

Cream cheese and redcurrant jelly

Cottage cheese with avocado and lemon juice

Cheese and chutney

Grated cheese with grated apple and pear

Plain fromage frais and raisins

Chopped hard-boiled egg, water-cress and mayonnaise

Egg mayonnaise with a little curry powder

Chopped hard-boiled eggs with mashed sardines

Tuna mayonnaise and salad cress

A small can of tuna or salmon with 3 tablespoons tomato ketchup

Tuna or salmon salad

Canned salmon, chopped egg and mayonnaise

Chopped chicken, mayonnaise and yoghurt with a little curry powder and raisins

Chicken or turkey with chutney

Grilled chicken liver, mashed with fried onions and hard-boiled egg

Chocolate spread and banana

Open Toasted Sandwiches

Toast the bread first, then spread with the topping and put under a hot grill until cooked.

Cheese and tomato

Grated cheese and apples with a few raisins

Canned sardines in tomato sauce

Chicken in béchamel sauce

TODDLER MEAL PLANNER

	Breakfast	Lunch	Tea	Dinner
Day 1	Fruity Swiss Muesli Yoghurt Fruit	Juicy Beefburgers and vegetables Apple Crumble and custard	Animal Pasta Salad with Multi-Coloured Vegetables Home-Made Ice Cream or frozen yoghurt	Miniature Sandwiches *Petit Suisse* Fruit
Day 2	Cheese on toast Fruit Compote	Grandma's Tasty Fish Pie Fruit	Top-Hat Egg Fruit	Chicken and Apple Balls and vegetables Snow-Covered Fruit Salad
Day 3	French Toast Apple Purée *Petit Suisse*	Veal Stroganoff and rice Baked Bananas	Gefilte Fish Balls with salad or raw vegetables in dip Fruit	Toasted sandwich Peach Melba Delight
Day 4	Mixed Cereal Muesli Scrambled egg	Tasty Peanut Rissoles Animal Jelly and Home-Made Ice Cream	Chicken and Apple Balls Snow-Covered Fruit Salad	Spaghetti Primavera *Petit Suisse* Fruit
Day 5	Raisin Bran Muffin Banana Split	Shepherd's Pie and vegetables Grandma's Lokshen Pudding	Fish in Creamy Mushroom Sauce Jelly Fruit	Tasty Peanut Rissoles Fruit Yoghurt
Day 6	Cornflakes with Apple Yoghurt Fruit	Tuna Tagliatelle Fruit	Liver Casserole and vegetables Tea-Time Apple Treat	Miniature Sandwiches *Petit Suisse* Fruit
Day 7	Cheese Scramble and toast Fruit	Bar-B-Q Chicken or Stir-Fried Chicken Apple Crumble and Home-Made Ice Cream	Stuffed Potato Jelly Fruit	Gratin of Sole Ratatouille *Petit Suisse*

These meal charts show you how to plan ahead and cook for the whole family together.

FAMILY MEAL PLANNER

	Breakfast	*Lunch*	*Dinner*
Day 1	Fruity Swiss Muesli Yoghurt	Animal Pasta Salad with Multi-Coloured Vegetables	Juicy Beefburgers, vegetables and potato Apple Crumble and custard
Day 2	Cheese on toast Fruit Compote	Chicken and Apple Balls and vegetables	Grandma's Tasty Fish Pie and vegetables Snow-Covered Fruit Salad
Day 3	French toast	Tasty Fish Pie or Gefilte Fish Balls with salad Fruit	Veal Stroganoff with rice and salad Home-Made Ice Cream or yoghurt and fruit
Day 4	Scrambled egg	Tasty Peanut Rissoles or Gefilte Fish Balls or Chicken and Apple Balls Fruit salad	Spaghetti Primavera Tasty Peanut Rissoles Jelly and Home-Made Ice Cream
Day 5	Raisin Bran Muffins	Fish in Creamy Mushroom Sauce and vegetables	Shepherd's Pie and vegetables or salad Grandma's Lokshen Pudding
Day 6	Cornflakes and Yoghurt	Tuna Tagliatelle Fresh fruit	Liver Casserole and potato Tea-Time Apple Treat and Home-Made Ice Cream
Day 7	Cheese Scramble Toast and Fruit	Bar-B-Q Chicken or Stir-Fried Chicken and Vegetables Apple Crumble and Home-Made Ice Cream	Gratin of Sole Ratatouille

INDEX

Page numbers in light type denote additional recipes containing the given ingredient

ACKNOWLEDGEMENTS

I am indebted to the following people for their help and advice during the writing of this book.

Dr Stephen Herman FRCP, Consultant Paediatrician, Central Middlesex Hospital.
Margaret Lawson, Senior Lecturer in Paediatric Nutrition, Institute of Child Health.
Professor Charles Brook, Consultant Paediatric Endocrinologist, Middlesex Hospital.
Dr Sam Tucker FRCP, Consultant Paediatrician, Hillingdon Hospital.
Jacky Bernett, Community Dietician.
Dr Tim Lobstein, specialist in children's food and nutrition at The London Food Commission.
Carol Nock SRN FCN, Midwife.

Kathy Morgan, State Registered Health Visitor.
My mother, Evelyn Etkind, for all her encouragement in writing this book.
David Karmel, for his patience in teaching me how to use a computer.
Beryl Lewsey for her enthusiasm and hard work.
Ros Edwards, Ian Jackson, Susan Fleming, Fiona Eves and Elaine Partington of Eddison Sadd.
Dr Irving Etkind, for his help in research.
Jane Hamilton, my nanny, for restraining my children from wiping out my manuscript on the computer!
And, most important of all, my husband Simon, my chief guinea pig, for all his support.

The Author

Annabel Karmel is a busy working mother with two small children, Nicholas and Lara. Her fascination for food was stimulated by studying at the Cordon Bleu School of Cookery and, since the birth of her children, she has thoroughly researched all aspects of feeding babies and children, to cut through the often confusing and conflicting advice given to mothers on the subject. A classically trained harpist, Annabel has had a glittering musical career. At the age of sixteen, she won a scholarship to the Royal Conservatoire of Music in the Hague and subsequently studied at the Royal College of Music in London, but it was through light, popular music recitals that Annabel really made her mark. She is also a singer and an actress and has made numerous television appearances. Annabel lives in London with her husband, Simon, and family.